Nagarjun Nagesh

THE ART OF BUILDING YOUR WEALTH

Four Personal Financial Strategies To Implement For Millennials

THE ART OF BUILDING YOUR WEALTH

Table of Contents

Prerequisites For Building Your Wealth   13
1. Expectation
2. Why The Rich Get Richer
   - 2.1. Leverage
   - 2.2. Ignorance
   - 2.3. Your First Million Is The Hardest
3. Are You Rich If You Own A BMW?
   - 3.1. Used Vehicle Prone Shopper (Uvps)
   - 3.2. The Man Who Sold His Real Estate
   - 3.3. Property To Buy A Car
4. Is Your Home An Asset Or A Liability?
   - 4.1. Home Is Your Security
   - 4.2. What Is Worse Than Paying A
   - 4.3. Mortgage Towards The Home
   - 4.4. You Are Living In?
   - 4.5. Should You Sell Your Home?
   - 4.6. What About A House Or A Real Estate?, How Should You Buy The Properties?

Finding Your Purpose   32
5. Where Should We Begin?
   - 5.1. Definiteness Of Purpose
   - 5.2. What's Your Story?
   - 5.3. Plan
   - 5.4. Action
   - 5.5. Discipline
   - 5.6. Overcoming Myopia
6. Find Your Desire For Financial Freedom
   - 6.1. Significance
   - 6.2. Growth
   - 6.3. Security

- 6.4. Contribution / Love
- 6.5. Epitome Of Financial Illiteracy
7. Find What Drives You To Achieve
    - 7.1. Outliers
    - 7.2. Passion
    - 7.3. Value
    - 7.4. Desires Of A Laptop Technician
8. Self-motivation! A Necessity For Success
    - 8.1. Increase Your Ability To Earn
    - 8.2. Enough
    - 8.3. Contribution
    - 8.4. Draining All Of Your Will Power
9. Self-analysis! Understanding Your Habits
    - 9.1. Environment
    - 9.2. Nurture
    - 9.3. Habits
    - 9.4. The Girl Who Taught Me How To Spend Strategically
10. Include Your Partner Or Get A Prenup
    - 10.1. Synchrony
    - 10.2. Individualism
    - 10.3. Prenup
    - 10.4. One Builds; The Other Destroys!
    - 10.5. Divorce
    - 10.6. The Financial Conversation
11. The Power Of Dreaming!
    - 11.1. What If I Am Really Comfortable
    - 11.2. Where I Am?
    - 11.3. How Do You Become Successful In Life?
    - 11.4. Does Providing Value Make You Successful?
    - 11.5. The Real Price Of Not Doing What You Love

Income Management Strategy   87

12. Do You Really Need A Budget To Become Financially Free?
    12.1. Going Over The Budget
    12.2. Alternate Way To Spend
    12.3. Losing The Purpose To Budget
13. I Cannot Save A Penny More!
    13.1. Create A Budget
    13.2. Latte Factor
    13.3. Bring In More Money
    13.4. Clear Cut Strategy
14. Income Allocation Strategy
    14.1. Wealth Builder
    14.2. What's Worse?

Debt Management Strategy   108
15. Emergency Fund: Why Is It Important?
    15.1. Credit Cards
    15.2. Comfort Zone
    15.3. A Series Of Unfortunate Events
16. Debt Analysis: Analysing Your Financial Past?
    16.1. Credit Card Debt
    16.2. Education Loan
    16.3. Home Loan
    16.4. Car Loan
17. Debt Management Strategy
18. Credit Cards: How To Increase Your Credit Score
    18.1. Do I Need A Credit Card?
    18.2. Danger!
    18.3. Cash Is Still The King!
19. Home Loan: Is It A Boon In Disguise?
    19.1. Setting A Realistic Goal
    19.2. Can You Get It Right?
    19.3. Home Loan
    19.4. Housing Bubble

Savings Management Strategy   **148**

20. Savings Management Strategy
    - 20.1. Saving To Spend
    - 20.2. Short Term Investment
    - 20.3. Midterm Investments
    - 20.4. Long-term Investments
    - 20.5. The Friend Who Lost His Lifetime Savings
21. Mark Zuckerberg Didn't Save His Way To Financial Freedom
    - 21.1. Did You Know That A Third Of The
    - 21.2. Lottery Winners Declare Bankruptcy?
    - 21.3. Compounding
22. How To Save Your Way To Achieve Your Dream
    - 22.1. Invest In Yourself
    - 22.2. Expanding Your Streams Of Income
    - 22.3. Paying Less Tax
    - 22.4. Saving More By Cutting Spending
    - 22.5. Doubling Down On What Works For You
    - 22.6. Planning To Achieve Your Dream
    - 22.7. Grass Is Greener On The Other Side
23. Buying A Car The Right Way
    - 23.1. Why Shouldn't You Pay For The Car
    - 23.2. With A Loan?
    - 23.3. Comfort And Prestige
24. Never Kill Your Golden Goose
    - 24.1. Burden Of Debt
    - 24.2. Ball And Chain
    - 24.3. Destruction In Disguise
    - 24.4. Misery Loves Company
    - 24.5. Can Someone Be Comfortably Broke?
    - 24.6. Paying For Your Comfort Zone

25. Financial Goals To Achieve Before You Turn 35
    25.1. Being Paid For Your Value
    25.2. Have A Full Fledged, Practising
    25.3. Personal Financial Plan
    25.4. Having Saved 6 – 12 Months
    25.5. Worth Of Income As Emergency Fund
    25.6. Dedicating A Portion Of Your Income Towards Your Retirement
    25.7. Having Multiple Sources Of Secure
    25.8. Income

Investment Management Strategy   **209**
26. Investment Management Strategy
27. Investing In Mutual Funds
    27.1. Why Have People Interested In Mutual Funds?
    27.2. What About Others Who Save For
    27.3. The Retirement With The Mutual Funds?
    27.4. Mutual Fund Nominal Returns Vs
    27.5. Real Returns
    27.6. Why Do We Calculate
    27.7. Inflation-adjusted Returns Instead Of
    27.8. Nominal Returns?
    27.9. Comparison Of After-tax Returns
    27.10. Should You Invest In A Mutual Fund?
28. Investing In Index Funds
    28.1. The Best Index Fund
    28.2. Tax Exemptions In India
    28.3. Vanguard 500 Index Investor (VFINX)
    28.4. Comparison Of Funds
    28.5. Peak
    28.6. How Could The Index Fund Be Used

    28.7.   To Aid In The Attainment Of
    28.8.   Financial Freedom?
29.   Investing In Fixed Deposits
    29.1.   Emergency Fund!
    29.2.   Catch Up With Inflation
    29.3.   Do You Know If You Could Get Your
    29.4.   Money Back If Banks Become Bankrupt?

Bibliography   **246**

Investment Advice Disclaimer   **250**

PROLOGUE

Any Economy is maneuvered by income & expenditure and assets & liabilities. Likewise even personal finance management need be addressed through quadruple strategies as elucidated by this promising book which has clearly spelt the itinerary for the financial journey. The book on your hands serves as a practical manual for Income Management, a blueprint for Savings Management, a short guide for Investment Management and a road map for Debt Management.

The following well known adage has its own latent connotations in this context.

> "If Financial Wealth is lost Nothing is lost.
>   This book will build for you if imbibed sincerely.
> If Financial Health is lost Something is lost.
>   This book will cure you, if practiced earnestly.
> If Financial Character is lost Everything is lost.
>   This book will discipline you, if adopted willingly."

The art of building your wealth has aptly driven home the genesis pattern of financial thoughts which eventually construct your financial destiny by explaining the following sequence.

"Watch your mental inputs and belief system.
Because they generate your financial thoughts.
Watch your thoughts.
Because they give rise to feelings and impact the financial behavior.
Watch your behavior.
Because it transforms to financial habits and character.
Watch your character.
Because it squarely defines and conclusively decides your financial destiny."

The author delivers completely practicable and refreshing ideas on how to create spectacular monetary well being and attract positive results through many of the amply tested tips a few of which are portrayed below.

1. The successful and down to earth recipe that promises attainment of financial goals is earn, save, invest and clone the process. Practice makes perfect and the trick to mastery is repetition. To accumulate the first million looks the hardest upon achieving which one is already on the accustomed track to grow bigger.

2. Working for a company merely for money will hardly bring the best out of an employee. It is "Pay well when you are served well" and "Do not rob Peter to pay Paul". Overpayment for an underperformance naturally renders an employee too expensive to afford for any company. Even when the employee hones himself to become indispensable for the

company, forces demanding survival of the financially fittest will still be at work to sabotage the progress and dislodge the status unless the needed financial soft skills are exhibited.

3. The first expenditure should be savings. The act of saving should happen impulsively without perceiving it as a control exercised on spending.Even as savings should precede spending , spending ought not to exceed earning. Being in debt signifies attention to the fact that one is earning little or spending more. It becomes necessary to create multiple streams of income even by acquiring new skills.It lacks prudence to satisfy current unrewarding desires assigning unpredictable future income.

4. The smart way to get rich is to budget the expenditure so as to buy income generating assets from the resultant savings invested in the process to fetch optimized returns. There is no point in deliberately choosing to be trapped by a readily available loan if the borrowed money can not generate more than what the repayment commitment turns out to be.

5. The process of financial literacy begins with building the emergency fund. In the event of being taken unaware by a series of unfortunate mishaps, such emergency fund dawns to the rescue by providing the much needed shock absorption to consciously have what one desires rather than be victimized by the draconian circumstances.

6. Self discipline is the trait to work pragmatically and continually towards a genuinely focused goal in order to achieve it and a man can become the best expression of himself if he loves what he does. While luck is what happens when preparation meets opportunity , the preparation itself is just the end product of motivation and perseverance. A comfort zone is a fool's paradise where nothing happens. Actions require efforts and effort has no locus standi in a comfort zone.

7. Evolving a definite purpose for each goal by awakening the giant within shields the boat of finance from drifting and enables heading for destination. When there is determination backed by passion to excel consistently, financial success will be the inevitable byproduct. Backing up the performance of the desirable act with reinforcement of sound reasons pre -empts giving up in the near or far future ending up living the way that was never intended to. It is wiser to deepen the roots and settle down in the right sphere if one does reasonably well already since indiscriminately rolling stone gathers no mass.

8. If the pre retirement experience is "Penny saved is a penny earned", the post retirement reality witnessed is "Penny spent is a Penny lost". Hence retirement plans should support and aim at maintaining the ongoing standard of living without any compulsion for a financial compromise.

This personal finance project book is a passport for better tomorrow and stretches the vision to earn a good living on self set terms once the secrets of success formula prescribed here are executed. Money like babies grows larger by nursing. It is open for everyone nursing drive, determination and perseverance to develop the personal financial skills vividly narrated in this book. It offers crucial insights at the turn of this millennium, to achieve financial goals and dreams with extraordinary results.

Making both ends meet and keeping head & shoulders above water have been scientifically formulated and customized by the author on simple cause and effect pattern. The author has indeed redefined financial happiness. Happiness is not merely a state of mind and a happy person is not the person living in a set of ecstatic circumstances. But a happy person is rather one endowed with a certain set of financial attitudes detailed in this book.

Get set to turn a new leaf and live your financial dreams.

Dr Nagesh Balasubramanian
Assistant General Manager
Nationalised Bank in India

Part One

Prerequisites for Building Your Wealth

Introduction

Expectation

"Do nothing, say nothing and be nothing and you'll never be criticized" - **Elbert Hubbard.**

Money, Love & Enemy...

These are some of the words which evoke extreme emotions.

Love is prevalent in the society. We learn to express them from the moment we are born. Nobody has to expressly teach us how to love. They are embedded in our DNA.

However the same cannot be told for money. Ask yourself what is money?

Ask others "What is money?" Everyone has a different explanation for it. Some say "Money is the root of all evil".

"The love of money is the root of all evil" - **Bible, 1 Timothy 6:10.**

Some are ashamed of not having enough money. Some are guilty of having a lot of money. Some are indeed greedy. There are as many emotions as there are emotions themselves which are expressed when money comes into play.

Some are willing to trade something more valuable than money like their family, health, happiness, etc as money has the power to create and destroy everything in its path.

> "Money is a good servant but a bad master"
> **- Sir Francis Bacon.**

What is money?

Can you imagine the times without money? Imagine yourself there wanting salt in an era without money. All you have is two bags of rice. When you go to the salt vendor he says "I already have enough rice mate, bring me two live chickens, I'll trade with you".

Things escalate quickly when the livestock vendor wants something else. It's such a pain!

Money liberates you from pain and provides the option to do whatever you want to do with it.

> "Money is freedom"

How you are willing to build the wealth is what differentiates one from the other. While choosing a title for this book, I was perplexed by the choice of using "The Art of Building Your Wealth". Building your wealth requires vivid imagination & skill and expresses important feelings and emotions. If building your wealth is not art what else is it?

Science is boring for many. Art feels beautiful & skillful. Only the experienced, well educated in the art of personal finance can even think of building their wealth. You'll see in the pages to come how to build your wealth from scratch.

I always feel if you want to become like someone find out how they achieved it and follow their path. You will reach there all by yourself.

Having been perplexed with the same questions and spending quite a couple of years learning about the successful people I stumbled upon an important factor common with all the successful ones.

We all remember them for the work which they do without that they are nobody. What comes to your mind when I say Elon Musk, Warren Buffett, Bill Gates, Tony Robbins, Mark Zuckerberg? Their contribution to this society is humongous and they are an immense success.

I've been studying them and this is what I have found. Although their work life has to do nothing with their personal life, it creates an opportunity for them to be successful. But wait, not all of them are Donald Trumps & Mike Tysons. They are in the top 1%. What about the remaining 99% of the population?

How can they be successful? Heck! I am in the 99%. If only the top 1% can be successful in life, we are all failures and I am too proud to declare it!

Success for most of us (Millennials) is building a home, buying a car, retiring with a lump sum of money while traveling around the world.

Knowing how to achieve these is half the battle won! I developed four simple strategies to implement in your life to make sure that you reach there and they are **Income, Debt, Savings & Investment Management Strategies.**

My promise to you is: If you choose to stick with me until the end, these four strategies have the power to help you reach your financial freedom.

I detest using the word win! As it brings the thought of losing to mind! If you win, someone else loses. We the 99% often lose! That's how we learn. But if you know the rules of money, you can keep making a decent amount of money for a really long time and retire rich.

When I say Sylvia Bloom, does it ring a bell? I am sure it doesn't. She was a frugal receptionist who made a whopping $12 million dollars by the time she died.

She did it the slow way, She did not earn the lottery or win something huge along the way. She learned the rules of money and she applied it to her life.

You can make it too. Any normal person has the ability to do just that if he or she is willing to. Life is full of opportunities and those with a strong purpose and determination can achieve what Sylvia Bloom has achieved.

2

Why the Rich Get Richer

Certainly, the possibility of living in a civilized world develops the opportunity for inequality.

The opportunists seize every opportunity to make a profit.

They deserve every single penny they make out of it while the others stay in ignorance of these opportunities.

There are two factors at play here:
1. Leverage
2. Ignorance

Though the opportunity was available to all of them, only the opportunist was able to see the opportunity at hand.

This is only made possible with the help of Leverage.

LEVERAGE

Leverage in simple terms is to **use something to a maximum advantage.**

Let's say that there is an opportunity to make money by cleaning a house. You could do it in a number of ways.

1. Use a plain old broom and a mop to clean the house (1 hour).
2. Use a vacuum cleaner to clean the house (30 min).
3. Use an automated robotic cleaner (Automated).

What does this mean financially?

1. You could spend one hour to clean the house *(Free)*.
2. You could hire someone to do it for you *($10.62 per hour)*.
3. You could also buy a vacuum cleaner to make it easier *($60 – $200)*.
4. You could buy an automated robotic cleaner *($200 – $1000)*.

Depending on your region and country, all these figures will vary but the point remains that you are saving time/money depending on what you are willing to choose.

1. If you prioritize your time, you would be choosing to hire someone to do the house cleaning for you (Human / Machine).
2. If you prioritize your money, you would be cleaning it yourself.

Leverages here are Vacuum Cleaner, Robotic Cleaners, and Man Power.

Let's take a financial example this time.

I have a $100 in my bank account and you have a $100 million in your bank account.

We both choose to invest it in a low-risk index fund which yields a moderate 8% annual return on investment.

After a year, My initial $100 would have become $108 while your $100 million would have become $108 million.

Even though we both had equal opportunity, you were able to make the most of the index fund investment.

What is the Leverage here?

Capital

To add insult to injury, I've earned all of my $100 while you have inherited your $100 million.

Now, I may feel life is unequal!

In reality, it is not.

Your parents may have worked hard and deserved every penny of what they have earned and then passed it on to you.

IGNORANCE

"Ignorance is bliss"

If you are unaware of an unpleasant situation, you cannot be troubled by it.

In the above-mentioned example of index fund investment. I would have been happy If I did not know that you made $8 million in the same transaction, doing exactly what I did.

Initially, the wealth gap between you and me was $99,999,900.

After a year, the wealth gap between you and me has widened to $107,999,892.

A classic example of **Rich getting richer, poor becoming poorer.**

While this fact is true, inflation is also catching up to eat up what I've earned in interest, along with tax payment to the government and costs involved with the fund.

The real return on investment could be anywhere between $2 – $6 while you could be looking forward to earning anywhere between $2 million to $6 million.

Your parents might have worked hard; learnt along the way to become the best in their fields to accumulate and provide you a $100 million. While mine did nothing and provided me with a total inheritance of $0.

It is in every parent's interest to ensure that their children have every bit of the advantage in this world.

The more developed the nation, the deeper the family legacy and inheritance. If you ensure that you increase the total family inheritance by say 20% in total over your lifetime and leave your children with a net inheritance of $120 million, you are essentially making sure that your family has an advantage in the capitalistic society we live in today.

Meanwhile, if I ensure that I spend every little penny that I have left and leave my children with a net inheritance of $0 I ensure misery to my children.

Again a classic example of **Rich getting richer, poor becoming poorer.**

What can we learn here?
1. The lesser the resources, the harder it is to save.
2. The more the money, the easier it is to save.
3. I spend everything which I earn and invest.
4. You could never imagine spending $8 million a year. So, you end up investing it again.

YOUR FIRST MILLION IS THE HARDEST

If you are determined enough and are motivated sufficiently. You will eventually earn your first million in the 30 + years of your career.

Always remember

Earn => Save => Invest => Repeat

It is the only recipe which promises the attainment of your financial goals.

But don't people who invest end up losing money?

These are the people who do not do their homework before investing.

Just like other industries, the Investment sectors are full of gold diggers. You must be aware of it and make sound investment decisions with the least risk.

In order to be aware of what makes an investment sound, you need to keep learning about the art of making money.

Be inquisitive; strive to learn; every little experience is a lesson on what works and what does not.

> "Ignorance is not bliss when it comes to investing."

It would generally take me 2 – 3 generations if I am lucky to get from where I am today to catch up with say $100 million net worth if everything goes right.

But if enough people like me think that inequality is the root of all evil and decide to revolt against it, maybe we can throw away the current government and manage to press the reset button on the inequality.

When the civilizations start building a society again, it is inevitable that the inequality will breed again.

According to Walter Scheidel, a professor of Roman History at Stanford University and the author of "The Great Leveler", there are only four factors which have the ability to reset the problem of inequality – **war, disease, State collapse and revolution.** But as soon as the devastation is over, income inequality builds again.

In the process of destroying inequality, we will risk destroying the whole civilization as we know it. Simply to start from the scratch again.

Do you really want to reset all the achievements that your country has gone through simply because you do not have the patience to wait until the money compounds to $100 million after 2 – 3 generations?

3

Are You Rich if You Own a BMW?

Can somebody be dead broke and still own a BMW? Yes, anybody can be dead broke and still own a BMW according to the book – "The Millionaire Next Door".

The majority of millionaires own their cars rather than lease. Approximately 1 in 4 hold the current years model but another 25% have a model that is a four-year-old model. What about the millionaires who buy used cars? 33% of millionaires in the US buy used cars.

So what about all the millionaires who buy BMW's? 68% of all the luxury car buyers are not millionaires. In fact, the facts say that the people who trade old cars for the newer model owe more in trade value than the market value. It is tough to get wealthy by doing stuff like that.

USED VEHICLE PRONE SHOPPER (UVPS)

The used vehicle prone sectors are 20% of all the millionaires. They are aggressive shoppers. They get the best deals by shopping amongst private owners, dealers and leasing companies. This segment recommends productive strategies which could be applied to all aspects of life. Their life style patterns, financial habits and their attitude towards life itself is different and is a must learn.

They are the most efficient sectors in transforming income into wealth than any other sectors of vehicle acquisition groups. As a result, this sector is most likely to hold a six-figure salary or more. Since the income is always in correlation to wealth accumulated they tend to be really wealthy.

The UVPS are savers and tend to spend a lot less than others. They are most likely to become Millionaires. People who are driving their BMW'S tend to be non-millionaires who live a high-income lifestyle. They are in a race and often tend to be extremely broke. They have to hold their current job to pay the monthly installments towards the BMW and their million dollars home and often do not have the savings to hold their current lifestyle even for one month.

Do you want to buy a BMW? A brand new one? Can you settle for a second hand BMW that's a decade old? Are you a UVPS?

THE MAN WHO SOLD HIS REAL ESTATE

PROPERTY TO BUY A CAR

While studying my master's in Coventry University, I used to live with 5 other friends of which 3 of them were really big fans of cars.

As far as I know, we all come from a middle class family who could not afford to sponsor our living expenses in UK with the income from India.

We have to work part time jobs to cover our expenses and occasionally request money from our family. There are others who either sell their property/home or mortgage their only home and come to UK in order to graduate.

1. I was fortunate enough to be sponsored solely from my father's income.
2. Jack came to Coventry after selling his real estate property.
3. Jim had to borrow the money from bank after offering his only home as a collateral.

What did they both do? Spend almost all the money funded for the education while not finishing the course.

Meanwhile, in order to ease their discomfort, Jack bought a car which was seized by the police during his journey to Cambridge for drunk and driving. He left the car in Cambridge because he could not afford to pay the £400 fine for his £550 car. Alas! He did not have any insurance on his car!

To put it into perspective, £550 was almost 1 and half months of expenses when we were living there as students. He came to UK with a net £7000 or 700,000 rupees.

The Rupee was really down during 2013. A 100 rupee was equal to £1. So, It was a hell lot of money! I never understood their intention of buying a car anyway let alone not completing the course.

There were an exceptionally high number of students from his locality who did not finish their course while studying in UK when compared to students from other cities. I could attribute all these to **personality, priority and lack of direction.**

Their priorities were enjoying the time in UK while it lasted never bothering to attend the classes.

Never be like Jack or Jim, they are both currently jobless and aimless.

Jim occasionally asks me for 5000 rupees through messenger and I am swift to say no for I know the money is not going to a better use.

4

Is Your Home an Asset or a Liability?

We call it home because we live there with our loved ones; else it is a house, a real estate property, an asset or a liability. Your financial planner / real estate agent calls your home an asset. But what is the difference between an asset and a liability in the first place? Is your home an asset or a liability? Well, you are going to pay a rent for the house you are living in if you do not own that house.

HOME IS YOUR SECURITY

Home can be categorized as a security. Home is the place you live in and it offers a secure place to stay. What else is categorized as a security? You need a place to live, you need food to live and you need clothes to wear. They are the most basic necessities. So buying a home where you live on a loan is also security. You are going to pay rent otherwise to somebody which is worse than paying a mortgage payment towards a home you live in.

WHAT IS WORSE THAN PAYING A MORTGAGE TOWARDS THE HOME YOU ARE LIVING IN?

Buying a home when the prices are really high and continuing to pay the mortgage until 8 years later when the home prices have dropped by 40 – 60%. That's painful! A lot painful than paying a rent. A situation which occurred in the US during 2008 housing crisis.

SHOULD YOU SELL YOUR HOME?

In an ideal world, you shouldn't sell your home. But people move from place to place and sometimes are forced to sell their home. So in such cases, buy a home in areas where the prices are really low.

You make money while buying and not vice versa. If you find a good bargain while buying a home and are not paying a huge sum of money as transaction fees and are not buying a flexible interest rate on the mortgage or a mortgage for 30 years you can buy that home.

WHAT ABOUT A HOUSE OR A REAL ESTATE?, HOW SHOULD YOU BUY THE PROPERTIES?

Robert Kiyosaki the author of "Rich Dad Poor Dad" is certain that a house is a liability.

It is a liability if you are paying to cover the expenses and you can convert it into an asset with the right kind of price for the real estate you are buying, with the right amount of loan repayment plan. We have to analyze if the place provides the appropriate income necessary for the repayment of the mortgage. If it does then we can buy the property from the place and make sure that it provides money into your pockets and not the other way around.

Sometimes saving for buying a home and waiting for the prices to drop in order to explain the expenses and the income is the right way to move forward. For example, During the 2006 and 2007 in US, home prices were increasing so fast that people could buy a house which was being built and sell it before completion for a profit. Such times will not last forever; as of 2008 the prices started falling; the tides changed for the worse with too many bad debts stacking up against the bankers; banks started failing and the government had to back them up. We all know how that turned out to be.

Buying a home requires a lot of research and patience. It requires a minimum savings of nearly 10 – 30% of the total value of the home, although paying the full amount is the ideal case scenario. Ask yourself, is this house a liability or an asset? Is the property putting money in my pocket or taking it away from me?

Part Two

Finding Your Purpose

5

Where Should We Begin?

We all have to start from wherever we are today. But to be financially successful where do we start from? Let's find out, Which statement resonates with you?

1. I am already doing whatever it takes but could barely get through life.
2. I live a darn good life and don't want to think about financial success.
3. I have a million dollars! A billion dollars! Invested in a long-term passive income stream yielding 14% a year.

Our limiting beliefs demotivate us from achieving, Our ego doesn't let us accept the reality, find out where you are now and accept the facts. Now it is time to take action. Why don't we begin with simple actionable steps?. Let's see.

DEFINITENESS OF PURPOSE

If there is one thing that you could adopt from this book it would be this.You need a definite purpose for every goal; without a purpose we will be like a boat drifting along the sea without a destination. Why do you want to be financially successful? What is the drive that motivates you to take action? Don't have a definite drive to motivate yourself to take action? "Find your drive!".

We will be discussing about them in *Chapter 6 : Find Your Drive For Financial Freedom.*

WHAT'S YOUR STORY?

The story that you build around the motive to be financially successful is what is driving you to achieve and if you build a strong enough story that you constantly keep thinking about, it is one step closer to achieving success.Everyone would love to be financially successful. What is it that sets the ones who actually achieve financial success apart? Often the financial success is a byproduct of a successful career or business. The career success or business success is a by-product of opportunity and preparation. Don't ever subscribe to the thought that it is pure luck. The preparation is a by-product of motivation and perseverance. Motivation and Perseverance are derived from reason. The reason is derived from the story you tell yourself.

> "Luck is what happens when preparation meets opportunity" – **Seneca, A Roman Philosopher.**

What is your story? Do you want to be financially successful because you wanted to be significant in life? Do you want money to grow to provide food and shelter for your family? As Tony Robbins in "Awaken The Giant Within" put it – "Everything that we do, we do for a reason. Everything we do is due to a need to avoid pain or to gain pleasure".

What is your pain or pleasure that is motivating you to move towards the financial success dream?

PLAN

With purpose sternly in place, what is the plan that you have right now that will move you towards the financial success dream? The natural outcome of definiteness of purpose is motivation and passion to achieve the dream. Utilize the motivation to plan the path which you would love to take. People are their best expression of themselves when they do what they love. It is extremely hard to be successful at what you do when you hate what you are doing.

Learn to love what you are doing. Become extremely good at it, better than anyone else in your field. Have the confidence to acknowledge the dream.

I do not know what to plan for! I am not sure if I will achieve what I am planning for. What do I do? Continue reading...

> "Dream is not that which you see while sleeping. It is something that does not let you sleep" – **A P J Abdul Kalam.**

ACTION

Having a definite purpose in life and a plan to achieve your dream will lead you to automatically take massive action.

Are you a procrastinator? Let us have a look at how to save more money for tomorrow. An awesome strategy implemented by Shlomo Benartzi. You can find the link below:

https://readorb.com/save-more-tomorrow/

Check the services provided by him on saving more tomorrow. He provides a way for all the US citizens to save more tomorrow and automate the process by saving a set percentage of their increments to invest and by the end of few years everybody who has enrolled in the programs starts saving 14% of their income. We definitely need one in India.

There are techniques which yielded great wealth to the man in the ancient city of Babylon by simply saving one-tenth of what he has earned for his future and his family.

> "Gold cometh gladly and in increasing quantity to any man who will put by not less than one-tenth of his earnings to create an estate for his future and that of his family" – **The Richest Man in Babylon by George Samuel Clason.**

DISCIPLINE

"Self-discipline is your ability to systematically and progressively work towards a goal and achieve it" - **The Neuropsychology of Self Discipline by Sybervision.**

Discipline to continuously strive and complete the journey take continuous action till the dream is achieved. What will I do if I am not disciplined enough? We can change it, we will cover the topic later. Are you particularly interested in automating your success and never having to worry about it?

As David Bach says "Who has the discipline to continuously save for years? Automate the process!". For those of you who would like to automate the process of saving & investing, "The Automatic Millionaire" by David Bach is the answer. Let's analyze it in the coming chapters.

OVERCOMING MYOPIA

How could my myopia have anything to do with personal financial freedom? It doesn't. However, it has got everything to do with purpose, planning, taking action and being disciplined.

A young dumb and 18-year old version of me thought "Studying in less light might make my eyes stronger". Continuing to do so for about a year, I found out that I could no longer see the blackboard in the classroom.

I can vividly remember the terrifying experience of no longer being able to see clearly. I reported that to my class teacher, who suggested me to wear glasses. Without a doubt, I was diagnosed with myopia -0.75 in my right eye and -1.00 in my left eye way back in 2008.

Fast forward to 2016, I have a -1.75 in the right eye and -2.00 in the left eye. Up until then, I was cool with wearing glasses and identified myself as a person wearing glasses.

I remember reading the book, "Spontaneous evolution: our positive future" by Bruce Lipton and had a revelation for the first time in my life. I knew something was wrong with wearing glasses. If I had a fever, Doctor would prescribe some medicine and the fever would go away in a few days.

Why doesn't the same happen to myopia? I thought maybe glasses were contributing to the increase in myopia. To my surprise, I found some websites like Endmyopia which motivated people to remove their glasses if they have a low prescription.

What was the downside? It takes years to reverse myopia, Luckily, I had developed myopia during my teenage and not previously. If I had developed it in my childhood, my eyeballs would have grown to accommodate for the spectacle power.

So, I removed my specs for the first time in my life on March 27, 2017.

Motivation - To reverse myopia and to be independent of glasses.

Purpose - I know wearing spectacles is being dependant on it forever, For some reason, I also felt having such a dependency would be a hurdle to propel me forward in my career path. I believed it strongly (I realize Sundar Pichai wears specs).

Plan - Remove the specs, Try to relax my eyes as much as possible and never wear it again.

Action - I put the specs away in my wardrobe and never touched it again.

Discipline - I never wore it again. Full stop.

As of July 30, 2018, my myopia has reduced from the previous -1.75 right eye and -2 left eye to -0.5 right eye and -1 left eye (Clinically Tested). A clear victory against progressing myopia. I am expecting to have myopia eliminated by 2020.

If I had never imagined that wearing spectacles would make me look a little more dependent than others who do not wear spectacles, I would never have done this experiment in the first place.

6

Find Your Desire for Financial Freedom

Why do human beings do what they do? Why do we need to be financially free? Some of them make a killing. Some sacrifice their life in the hope of providing a better life for their children.

People are pushed by needs. There are five needs which foster the desire for financial freedom. They are the most fundamental needs and everyone has a collection of these needs.

While the first three needs are the most abundant, people often find different means to achieve these needs. Joining the army and putting one's life in line for the nation or booking a whole IMAX theatre for $40,000 simply to prove to a person who left them seven years ago. Yes, it happened!

Let's have a look at the fundamental needs which foster financial freedom desires.

Five fundamental needs which foster desire for financial freedom are:

1. Significance
2. Growth

3. Security
4. Contribution
5. Love

SIGNIFICANCE

The significance is by far the most important need of all. People have the need to feel significant and having others to acknowledge that they are significant. It is the most primal need.

Even monkeys have them. There is always an Alpha Male in the tribe and most of the males fight for the position. Though we have evolved from them, these needs keep us up to date with the ever growing economy, improving technology and such other things.

> "To live intentionally implies that it is not going to be always convenient but it is what will take you to significance if you do not give up." — **Sunday Adelaja, "The Mountain of Ignorance".**

GROWTH

The second in the list is Growth. All businesses say the hardest thing to maintain is the success.

1. 90% of the companies fail in the first year.
2. 96% of the mutual funds fail in the first decade.
3. 99% of the companies vanish in a century.

We only remember General Electric, AT&T, don't we? What about Yahoo, Nokia, Enron? Do you still remember them? What about Motorola?

> "Out of your vulnerabilities will come your strength." — **Sigmund Freud.**

SECURITY

The third on the list is Security. The most fundamental need. The need to provide food and shelter for your family. Even though it is the most fundamental why is it in the third? The need for security can be fulfilled simply by needing to be significant or grow.

CONTRIBUTION / LOVE

The lack of ability to contribute can drive you crazy. We have the need to be more than what we can possibly be. We have accomplished a lot in the past century. We have abolished war, plague, and famine. We always had war, famine or plague. It wiped 2% to 20% of the population says Yuval Noah Harari in "Homo Deus: A Brief History Of Tomorrow". If you are in your 20's there is a 32% probability on an average that you will live till your 90's according to a business insider study. What are you going to do with your lives?

> "A rich life is lived from a giving heart, not a selfish mind." — **Rasheed Ogunlaru.**

EPITOME OF FINANCIAL ILLITERACY

Have you ever met anyone whom you consider to be a financial illiterate?

I did. Occasionally I would bring about financial topics which as you know, I love to speak about. I came to know that some people honestly have no interest to speak about finances and they delegated the task to their mom or dad.

But, this particular friend of mine was interesting as their family as a whole would delegate the task of financial money management to one of his uncles.

I was wonderstruck with this information. I had always believed that any human being is inherently selfish. I have never come across anyone yet who acts selflessly on such a consistent basis.

He was confident that his uncle was managing finance of all their families forever! His uncle, by the way, has his own family, kids, wife and is working to earn his share of income which he spends for his family.
Apart from this. He takes care of all the financial planning of my friends family. My inner instinct sensed something was clearly wrong!

"Every man for himself"

I never gave much thought to it next time and honestly, it was none of my business. My friend would never be bothered to know about finance. He was working with me in Spain as I recommended him.

One fine day, I asked him how he is managing all his finances. He told me that he is taking some advice from his uncle and following his lead.

My friend was earning as much as I was and I knew as a matter of fact that it was the first time that he was earning that much in his lifetime. He was only 24 years of age at that time.

Curious to know more about his uncle's advice on investing, I asked him what was it that his uncle suggested.

He said "My uncle suggested me to invest in a Chit Fund and I have been doing that since long before I came to Spain"

I was shocked. I have never heard of it in my entire life.

Later, I came to know it is a kind of savings and credit association system. It is a scheme which is organized by financial body or informally among friends.

How it works

Let's assume that 10 people have gathered to organize a chit fund with an organizer. Usually, the organizer does not participate in the chit fund.

Let's also assume that every person has to pay a sum of 20,000 rupees for 10 months. So, every person would be investing 200,000 rupees in the chit for a period of 10 months.

First month, all the 10 subscribers place their first month installment of 20,000 rupees in a pot. The organizer then auctions the money to the 10 subscribers. Any body who bids the lowest amount will receive the first months sum of 200,000 rupees. Let's assume that 1st subscriber has won the auction by bidding the lowest 170,000 rupees.

The organizer would then hand the 1st subscriber with 170,000 rupees and distribute the remaining 30,000 rupees after deducting a small percentage fee as his service charge.

Anyone who is too desperate for the money would bid the lowest and gain access to a lump sum money immediately after which they would continue paying the chit till the end of the tenure *(i.e 9 more months).*

The first subscriber has invested 200,000 rupees and received 170,000 rupees. The remaining 30,000 rupees is considered as the premium fee for early access to the lump sum money.

Risk

He finishes explaining everything and the first thing I ask him is what happens if someone defaults after obtaining the lump sum money.

He was participating in a 20 member chit fund for a period of 20 months and it was informal. Meaning, no one can do anything if the organizer/subscribers default on the payment.

What is the advantage of an informal chit fund! **Tax...**

You do not have to pay any taxes on the interest rates obtained.

My friend being a patient chap as he is, chose to wait till the end of the 20 month tenure to receive the payment from the organizer.

Only after the 20 months, the organizer offered to pay him the full amount 400,000 rupees in cash. My friend was currently in Spain and the organizer was back in India. My friend asked the organizer to pay a set amount by electronic transfer every month.

My friend received a total payment of 180,000 rupees in total and the remaining 260,000 rupees is nowhere to be seen. He might get the money in the next few months or years or he may not.

Only time knows the answer to this question. **Let's analyse this situation financially.**

He paid a total of 349,000 rupees and is scheduled to receive an amount of 400,000 rupees. A total rate of return of 12.75% for a period of 20 months.

What if he paid 20,000 rupees every month as a recurring deposit to a bank in India. How much could he have earned?

Paying for a period of 20 months, he would have earned a total sum of 424,488 rupees. A net profit of 24,488 rupees compared to the profit he earned from chit fund which is 51,000 rupees.

Chit fund offers a huge return, exactly 208% more than the recurring deposit as the recurring deposit only offers a return of 6.75% per annum.

> "Recurring Deposit is a special kind of Term Deposit offered by banks in India which help people with regular incomes to deposit a fixed amount every month into their Recurring Deposit account and earn interest at the rate applicable to Fixed Deposits" - **Wikipedia.**

Clearly, chit fund wins. The risk of getting the money as promised relies solely on the dedication of the subscribers and continuous participation of the organizer.

My friend clearly trusted the organizer too much and the organizer ended up spending my friend's 280,000 rupees. Now, my friend is in trouble. There is no proof that the organizer owes my friend his 280,000 rupees. Incase, the organizer wishes to default on the payment, there is absolutely nothing which my friend could do.

My friend contacted his uncle and still could not successfully retrieve all the money from the organizer.

Second mistake my friend did was the fact that he did not know any of the subscribers nor the organizer. That was too much of a risk. There is no emotional or financial obligation from the subscriber or the organizer to keep their end of the bargain.

Third mistake my friend did was delegating personal finance to his uncle who happens to have his own family and there by having his own separate personal financial obligations which will prove to be an extremely expensive mistake for my friend and his family.

If he had spent the time to find his financial freedom desires, he could have deposited the money in the recurring deposit which is risk free thereby receiving the promised capital + interest earned instead of investing in a chit fund which has a higher risk.

There is no use investing in a fund which provides a higher rate of return for a higher risk, as the risk of losing the capital invested is not tolerable in any circumstances.

Taking control of your financial freedom is the key to financial success. Expecting others to take control of your financial life while leading you to success is just wishful thinking.

Such scenarios are just a pipe dream. Your desire to attain your financial freedom has to have some meaning to you. It is your dream, your purpose and you should be the one attaining it. When it comes to personal financial success the journey itself is as important as the destination.

The journey towards your personal financial success will teach you some life lessons which will be useful for a lifetime. Having said that, It is not a surprise that the lottery winners go bankrupt a few years after winning millions of dollars.

If you do not know how to save or to multiply the money with a solid reason for the money to stay with you, certainly **you will end up wasting the money** on things which you do not need for a ridiculous price.

7

Find What Drives You to Achieve

Let's find out what drives us to achieve. A good number of people do the jobs they do not love to earn the riches they desire. If you have just enough determination, passion and desire to achieve and consistently outperform, financial success will be the byproduct. But we all know the person who works for more than 10 hours a day.

There are two perspectives to look at it. Either they are not efficient at finishing the work within the stipulated time or they are extremely good at what they do. Hence the manager prefers the hard worker to do the heavy lifting. The former might get fired and later might get to stay in the same position for years. What? Being extremely efficient is not enough to prosper? The fact is that the employee is more valuable to the business where he is. So how to prosper at work/business? Become an outlier!

OUTLIERS

"Outliers: The Story of Success" by Malcolm Gladwell holds some of the answers we need to find our drive. Malcolm analyses the success of Bill Gates and the rock band Beatles. The ability to gain 10,000 hours of practice at a very young age when the computers could only be found in universities is what led Bill Gates to success.

Apart from intelligence, talent also plays a role in the success many people hold. The key point here is the determination and the motivation to learn is what lead Bill Gates to gain the 10,000 hours of practice at a very young age.

It takes approximately a decade to gain the practice time mentioned above. Do you have the determination and the drive to do what you love and stay on course for a decade to start becoming an outlier?

PASSION

What is the job that you would love to do? The one thing which makes you look forward to tomorrow. Have you ever jumped out of the bed the next day morning looking forward to doing something? What is that? That's one of the things you are really passionate about.

To become truly successful never do anything just for money; do it with love. Find the career which you are passionate about.

> "You need passion to overcome obstacles and setbacks in life" – **"Think Big and Kick Ass" by Donald Trump and Bill Zanker.**

Do what you love most; do it till you get 10,000 hours of practice. Provide value along the way. After all being passionate about playing video games is not providing value to others.

The ability to monetize on your passion is a skill to master. **Be valuable to others in a field which you are passionate about with more than 10,000 hours of practice and people will die to work with you or be your customer.**

> "The only person you are destined to become is the person you decide to be." – **Ralph Waldo Emerson.**

VALUE

Become more valuable to others. Providing value is at the core of being successful. Do 100% of your current job and 50% of your boss' job to grow to the next level in your career.

What do I do if I am running a business? Be more valuable to others than anyone in your field. Provide more in usage value to others. Be the best in your field. Constantly strive to provide value.

> "Strive not to be a success but rather to be of value" – **Albert Einstein.**

DESIRES OF A LAPTOP TECHNICIAN

In India, sometimes we do not get what we want in our lives. I always wanted to be a software engineer.

Back in 2008, during my high school, I was really good at computer science. I would often solve all the problems proposed by the teacher and would always rank first in the exams.

We were given an opportunity to choose our university degrees. I wanted to take B.E in IT and was pretty stern about it. My parents thought that enrolling me in B.E Electronics and Communications Engineering would be a better option! Yes! Such things happen in India; I am not sure where else but definitely in India.

My parent's arguments were that choosing ECE would broaden my horizons and possibilities of landing at a lucrative job after graduation. They were right. I was offered a job at Cognizant Technology Solutions. It was a dream for me. I always wanted to work for CTS and was planning on joining it. I thought my life was settled. An uncle of mine is working for CTS for the past 16 years. Who could ask for something more right? I did.

After getting an offer letter from CTS which I was eagerly waiting for since my first year in college and after attaining the goal, the fun was finally over. I wanted more; so I applied for masters in the UK and got that too.

Why did I apply? I wanted to see the other end of the world and know what's out there! The initial visa for the education in the UK is one year and four months. I loved the change in the culture and the freedom which the UK had offered. By all means, I considered myself a successful graduate. All of my friends except a handful have flunked and have returned to their home countries.

My visa was due to expire in the next few months. I wanted more of UK; so I applied for an MBA course in London; I had no intention of completing it. It was supposed to provide me with enough time to search for a job in the UK. Meanwhile, I got a fulltime job as a laptop technician in Coventry.

Staying in the UK and experiencing the newly obtained freedom had obstructed my vision spectacularly. I wasted more than 8 months searching for a job while also being a laptop technician.

I had all the right intentions to do my best as a laptop technician in Coventry but my heart was always towards obtaining a corporate job as a control systems engineer or better a software engineer.

This prevented me from being the best expression of myself as a laptop technician. Even though I thought I was doing the best, I could hardly satisfy the owner. During the six months, I topped up once to a wrong number for a customer costing the company £20.

To put it into perspective, it was half of my daily income, then. I proved to be an expensive bargain for the mobile shop. So, they had to let me go after 6 months. I truly felt that I was not worthy of obtaining a corporate job. If I cannot work and satisfy a mobile shop owner, how could I truly satisfy a multinational company?

Later, I was offered another Graduate Software Engineer job in Kings Lynn. Just what I wanted. So, I borrowed a total sum of £1500 from my parents to migrate from Coventry to Kings Lynn.

Life suddenly became colorful. I was motivated to do whatever best I could do and to be my best. For the first few months, the company wanted me to be in the production line, actually manufacturing the product.

I gladly accepted it. All, I wanted was a job and honestly if I can be a graduate software engineer it did not matter. They knew very well that I just graduated from the university and did not have any experience as a software engineer.

I proved to be too expensive for the company as the company could hire the same talent for 30% less salary. The UK would not allow me to be hired for such a low salary as it is a prerequisite to obtain my visa. So, I had to be let go off!

"Don't ask me, didn't the company already know?" I was either too naive or they utilized me big time. I paid for the visa; I paid for migrating the house. Honestly, they had nothing to lose.

"I got fired again! Wow! I am truly unworthy". I convinced myself that the UK did not want me there. So, I had booked a one-way ticket to India. I did not want to waste another 8 months looking for a job and waste my parent's money.

After finding a job in India, I wanted to be valuable to the organization. The company took me as an unpaid intern. So, I learned different programming languages during my training. Finally, I thought of myself as worthy of working in a software industry since I was starting to get ahold of what programming actually is. Just then, the company with which I was working became bankrupt and everyone in the company was let go!

Fantastic! The world is conspiring against me. Why can't I hold a job for more than a year?

Lessons learned so far:

1. **If you work for a company just for money, you will never be able to be the best expression of yourself.** You will be fired for underperformance. You will also be unhappy while working there.
2. **If you are overpaid for your underperformance, you will become too expensive for the company** and they would have to let you go; even if it is the only job which you wanted all your life. Unless you are valuable and be more valuable than what they are actually paying you. You are not worthy!
3. **Even after you become valuable, the world around you could conspire against you** and throw you to trash. Don't think the world has ended!

All these were the best things that could ever have happened to me. They were the most valuable lessons which life could teach me.

If I am not worthy, no company would keep me there. I would be fired immediately. So, I constantly strive to learn and be on top of all the technologies.

I always ensure that my manager is happy with my performance and strive to improve and deliver better.

8

Self-Motivation! A Necessity for Success

Self-Motivation. Some time that is the only thing you will have in order to push yourself towards success. Waking up everyday feeling that you are causing a positive change in other people's lives and making it better for everybody as a community can be a motivator. Purpose can be the biggest motivator in times of hardship.

> "Man belongs to where he wants to go" – **David Schwartz.**

What can be more motivating than the purpose itself? The money that it reaps! It gives you the sense of fulfillment but getting the same amount of money for years together can be demotivating as well. As a human being, we either grow or die. Growth is the most important factor in everybody's life. How do we increase our ability to earn more money?

INCREASE YOUR ABILITY TO EARN

1. You need a strength of purpose to secure more money.
2. Increase your ability to work and your productivity.

3. Keen minded men look for progress and opportunities. They do not stand still, else they know they will be left behind.

The hope of growth and the need to make more money often make us think, "What is all this for?" When should I say what I have done is enough! After all, Warren Buffet is 87 years old and John C Bogle is 88 years old as of 2017 and they haven't stopped.

ENOUGH

If you are not happy along the way towards success, why does it matter? Sometimes you have to wait for your loved ones to grow along with you.

Give them the opportunity and the freedom to do so with your newly acquired wealth; else you will leave behind everyone and grow to be an extremely successful lonely man.

> "Success is not the key to Happiness. Happiness is the key to Success" - **"Enough"**, John C. Bogle.

Money makes us happy but the happiness which we experience rarely persists. Speaking and connecting with others provides lasting happiness when compared to the money. Without your loved ones around you, success and money mean nothing.

> "The great game of life is not about money it is about joining the battle to renew our community, our nation, and the world. To

make it better for everybody in the present and future to live a better and fulfilling life"
- "**Enough**", **John C. Bogle.**

We can all learn to be happy first by living a purposeful and meaningful life and by making others around us happy by giving. After all, isn't giving loving?

CONTRIBUTION

The most selfless of all the needs in the path to becoming financially free is also the purest form of love. Contribution without expectation can be the greatest motivator. As Tony Robbins in the book "Money - master the game" said: "All I had was $14 and I gave it all away to the little gentleman who treated his mother like a lady in the restaurant". It motivated him to achieve and be important in this life.

Now, Tony Robbins is worth millions of dollars. He still feeds a lot of people. He fed 100 million people recently. Of course with the help of others. It gives him a sense of purpose.

What is your motivation? Contribute today. Don't wait till you make more money. Providing one dollar to the needy is contributing.

DRAINING ALL OF YOUR WILL POWER

Have you ever experienced the feeling of giving up on your pursuit to something? That's the feeling of failure... Have you ever pushed yourself so hard to complete a task which you started?

While staying motivated to learn about personal finance, I've pushed myself too hard to complete a book by John C. Bogle - "Bogle on Mutual Funds".

The book was so dry and empty of emotions. No wonder they call him data devil. Any book which is void of emotion is a textbook of sort. It lacks the depth to connect with the reader but provides immense value to them.

I've learned as much as all the other personal finance books combined from Bogle on Mutual Funds. The value provided was immense but too daunting.

While reading a book, I do not just whoosh through it. I make sure to sustain as much knowledge as possible from the act of reading a book. I still vividly remember my motivation being drained slowly but steadily as I read through it.

As I finished reading half of the book, I realized that I didn't have any more motivation to read through it. I had to push myself to read the book very next day. It was daunting! It took me another 15 days to finish reading it.

Having used all of my willpower to finish reading, I never touched another book for a whole month and it took another two to three months to slowly start recovering from it. I had to re-motivate myself to start learning more about personal finance.

I swore to never do such a stupid thing ever in my life. I had wasted so much time not reading anything. I felt too low for not learning anything for one whole month. So I started learning about personal finance slowly.

Lesson learnt, **Never drain your willpower to do any act! Learn to motivate yourself to do instead.**

9

Self-Analysis! Understanding Your Habits

We were born helpless, unable to speak or feed ourselves on our own. The factors that influence who we become is to a large extent from the outside. Isn't it?

Yes but we all know the one person who despite all their circumstances succeeded to a large extent.

Take Nelson Mandela for example. He is known for as a non violent activist to prevent the anti-racist movements. In 1961, Mandela orchestrated a three-day national workers' strike. He was arrested for leading the strike and was imprisoned for the five years in prison. In 1963, He was brought to trial again and was imprisoned for life for political offenses and sabotage.

All of this was to abolish the racist ideology which was prevalent during his time. Oh! Yea, during his tenure, he also contracted tuberculosis for which he obtained comparatively poor treatment.

After receiving a Nobel Prize in 1993 for dismantling apartheid in South Africa, he became the first black President in 1994.

We do not have to go through what he had gone through; yet having the opportunity to grow, many of us settle down for far lesser than what we really deserve.

Let's have a look at what shapes us!

ENVIRONMENT

Does environment play a role in shaping you? Of course, it does.

There are 535 billionaires in the United States followed by China with 260 billionaires, that's half less than the United States.

Simply counting the number of billionaires can be misleading. Let's count the number of billionaires in proportion to the population. If we do that Monaco is the number one country with the population per one billionaire equal to 12,600. What about the United States? The United States grabs the thirteenth place with a population per one billionaire equal to 599,569.

Being born in United States for example provides a significant advantage over people being born in say, South Africa. Doing average in USA is equivalent to living a millionaire lifestyle in the developing nations.

However, "The Science of Getting Rich" by Wallace D. Wattles in 1910 argues that environment does not play a major role in shaping one's success. Wallace explains that getting rich is a not a matter of environment. If it were so then all the people from the same locality will be rich while the others would be poor.

He does agree that some environments may be much favorable than others.

What about talent then? Is it talent then which makes a man rich? But we can also find an extremely talented poor man. They are the most abundant in our generation.

What is the difference between the rich and the poor then? Rich people do things in a certain way. The way they do things in a certain way can be attributed to nurture, habit and character.

NURTURE

Immediate gratification! That's the crisis the Millennials are experiencing. How did it come to be? Immediate gratification is largely attributed to nurture.If you are the only child you are given everything that you want without having to experience rejection. We slowly become unable to face any rejection.

What are the effects of not being able to handle rejection or growing without experiencing any threat! You do not know how to handle these situations.

"Emotional Intelligence" by Daniel Goleman addresses these factors when he tells a story about a boy who was being harassed continuously by two bullies. Afraid that the bullies might hurt him, the boy brings his dad's handgun to school and kills the two bullies. When asked he said, "I was afraid they might hurt me".

Such extreme behaviors are attributed to the paralysing fear which the bullied experience.

What is the root cause of binging on food? Daniel Goleman says the root cause is the inability to understand if one is hungry, upset or angry. As strange as it may be it makes complete sense. How could it be avoided? People often grow up without understanding their inner world.

These scenarios can be avoided by teaching emotional intelligence at school.

> "Emotional intelligence is the ability to recognize, understand, label, express, and regulate emotions, both one's own emotions and those of others" – **Susan Rivers, Deputy Director, Yale University**.

HABITS

It's challenging to sit back and evaluate certain mindsets that you have developed over the past several years.

We often stick to our habits, either good or bad. The inability to evaluate oneself has become so common. We most likely develop these habits without being aware of it. How do you know if it is detrimental or beneficial to our long term success? By evaluating the world we live in and determining if the environment rewards you for the habit or punishes you.

"Habits either make you or break you"

What are the most beneficial habits to incorporate if we decide to get rid of old habits? People cannot simply stop doing something just because they have decided to. They have to replace the bad habit with a good habit. That is the only way out. The book by Stephen Covey – "7 Habits of Highly Effective People" has seven suggestions to offer.

1. **Be Proactive** – Being proactive is actively thinking about the action and consequences; then choosing to act in a way that would be constructive for the situation rather than choosing to react to a situation.
2. **Personal Leadership** – Be your own leader. Hold dominant thoughts in your mind to guide you. Let it serve as a beacon of light in times of darkness.
3. **Personal Management** – Learn to manage yourself effectively and efficiently, Anger management, for example.
4. **Seek Out to Understand; Then be Understood** – Become an active listener. Understand the underlying meaning and emotions of what other people say. Feel with them; then respond after they have finished.
5. **Win-Win Situation** – Always seek out a plan which will be mutually beneficial rather than

ripping somebody off which is a one-off Win-Lose Situation. Nobody likes to lose. Life is not a competition.
6. **Synergistic solution** – Learn to co-operate and work together. Working together can yield results of many folds. Two companies can join together and reach the heights they could never have achieved alone.
7. **Sharpen The Saw** – There are urgent – unimportant tasks, urgent – important tasks, not urgent – important tasks and not urgent – unimportant tasks. The first and the last have to be avoided at all costs, while the second task can be avoided by doing the third task proactively.

Uff! I know this chapter was a long one. But what about character? The character is your identity. Some say never change your Identity. I say it is at the root of Nurture that you develop your own character. If the nurture was not fruitful, it's time to change your character!

Always remember, your habits become your character and your character becomes your identity.

THE GIRL WHO TAUGHT ME HOW TO SPEND STRATEGICALLY

I never attributed myself as a personal finance expert while graduating from my bachelors back in 2012. I was well known to be a spendthrift.

Whenever I get a hold of money, I used to find a way to spend it all. When I possibly couldn't want anything, I would just waste it away.

What changed? Everything! The world as I knew it came crashing down on me when I began following my passion and joined Coventry University to pursue my masters in late 2012.

I was supposed to manage the household expenses for all the members of the house. Back in the beginning, we were only 3 people. One for every room. I was chosen to be the most responsible of all (LOL! I was by no means responsible).

I knew I wasn't even close to being responsible. But something changed. The responsibility of making sure all of us had enough food till the month ends changed me for some reason.

We used to allocate £60 per person and had a grand total of £180 to spend on groceries every month.

I spent all the money one week before the month ends to buy all the groceries during the first month. As embarrassing as it may be, I learned that monthly budgeted spending on groceries does not work, if I don't make sure that we spend in a controlled fashion every week, the effect of which could cost us one or two days of starving during the month end! You should see me by the end of four months! I have lost around 20 kilos.

Being poor at money management had a real effect on my health. I was dubious to manage the expenses on a weekly basis, mostly because we have become accustomed to this new impoverished lifestyle.

Maybe because the money management was already stressful enough, I didn't want to impose another layer of control over the expense.

Then, I met a girl who came to the UK to study at the start of the new year 2013. For some reason, she chose to trust me with managing all of her money. The worst possible person to trust was me, according to me. I also gave her all the reasons she should not trust me with all of her money. She still insisted that I take control of her expenses and just ensure that the money £7000 is sufficient for her to stay till the end of the year.

For the first time in my life, I was afraid to manage money. I knew that I am not perfect in money management and I did not deserve to manage someone else's money.

Heck! I couldn't manage my expenses. To make long story short, by October 2013, her account had a grand total of £0. Our agreement was that I made sure that the account would run dry by the start of the new year January 2014.

As expected, I failed again. Miserably this time. I had successfully proved that I was untrustworthy. Motivated to make things a little right, I started working full time as my masters ended by September 2013.

I would generate some £800 every month of which I would contribute some amount to her and ensure that she would only ask her parents around £200 every month. That's the best I could do then.

Finally, I started to learn the lesson on money management the hard way. The importance of money management dawned on me.

After all the series of events which unfolded, I wanted to not let another person down in my life, in case one chooses to trust me again.

I should say, I was by no means perfect after that and had failed multiple times later on as well. Just that, when things started to turn south, I learned from the money mistakes. It took another 4 years for me to become considerably better at money management.

10

Include Your Partner or Get a Prenup

Your partner is one of the most influential people in your life. The importance of having a right partner in life is realized in the emotional and financial aspect of your life.

With increasing equality towards women even in the developing nations, it is an eventuality that they will be treated equally to men around the world, a safer world where they have equal rights.

The developing nations are the most affected by the changing gender equality, being forced to accept the truth.

The world is becoming a safer place to live for both men and women. It is becoming a better place for the benefit of all of us. All the governments around the world are keen on promoting gender equality; so it is time for us to let them into our personal finance as well.

In the quest for more knowledge and wisdom, there is no room for male chauvinism and the similar beliefs preventing one from reaching the best expression of oneself.

So, having destroyed any room for male chauvinism to prevent one from including your partner in your endeavor to achieve financial freedom, we can speak about the advantages of including your partner.

SYNCHRONY

> "It is necessary to stay in synchrony financially and emotionally to make sure that the relationship pushes both of them to achieve."

The financial barrier is a hard nut to crack. Everyone has one's own priorities and wishes in life. After all, it is your earning and your savings; the one who is entitled is you, isn't it?

Who owns the relationship then? Is it you or is it she? The question is absurd, isn't it?

If you are in a relationship, it is equally taking part in it that makes it a relationship. Else I guess you can call it a dictatorship.

If you both equally love each other and trust that the bond will be lasting, it will not be hard to include the other half in your financial situation.

If you cannot trust them with your finance, don't trust them in the first place; why did you get married?

There is no room for selfishness in a relationship. If you have a child together, who owns the child? The child owns himself/herself.

You both play a role in shaping the child. You own nothing! Nothing except for the love that you share with your child and having the other half loving your child equally, as your child is equally hers.

You could create a financial situation from which you both could enjoy the benefits as long as you live and pass it on to your child after you are history.

INDIVIDUALISM

What is the point of living for yourself when the whole society is designed on how useful you are to others?

Do you want to pay for everything with money? Everybody in this society even your partner wants your money; don't they?

They will only want it as long as you say it is yours. When you develop a habit of sharing in your relationship, it is no longer yours but ours.

All these make sense when you are creating a stable financial situation together from scratch. But life is not always like that; Is it?

You have a legacy. You also bring your inheritance from your parents and their parents when you are marrying someone and getting into a long-term relationship.

What do you do with it as it is only yours? We have Prenups for that!

PRENUP

If you are already in a financially stable position when you meet your partner then it makes sense to get a prenup.

Even after getting a prenup, the society and the law can decide to throw the prenup out of the door and take the other partner's side.

These circumstances are becoming increasingly common as the divorce rates are increasing at a phenomenal rate.

This situation will put your financial situation in jeopardy. Better start the relationship thinking everything is ours so you won't have a financial and emotional shock if your partner decides to leave you.

For a good number of people, money governs their relationship, themselves and everything they do. These people are the ones that often break the relationships for money. They are also called Gold Diggers. It is relatively easy to find the gold diggers when you are an emotionally intelligent person.

Be a good judge of character. Spend time to nurture your relationship. Share the happiness. Experience life together.

If you cannot trust your partner with half of your finances, you are bound to live a stressful life.

ONE BUILDS; THE OTHER DESTROYS!

If you are already in a relationship where one has a surplus of money and the other is short on money, it is not uncommon to find one of them on a spending spree while the other tries to accumulate money.

A collaborative effort can take advantage of synergy and yield many times the result one could imagine achieving alone.

When you make the other person responsible for your money, they take pride in the ownership and try to preserve the current financial state.

Make sure you and your partner are on the same page when it comes to what you would like to do with the money that you both choose to save.

There is always an underlying reason when your partner is least bothered about the importance of saving. Convey how important it is for both of you to be secure financially and that relying solely on consumerism and borrowing for joy is a game which is bound to lead both of you to misery.

Start producing something together and find joy in generating money rather than consuming it. There are CEOs worth million dollars who have never borrowed a penny but own 100% of the company.

"Only Morons Start a Business on a Loan"
– **Mark Cuban.**

As life goes on, it either improves the relationship by building on trust or destroys the relationship. If you keep at it for long enough, you will either have an unbreakable trust or a broken marriage.

DIVORCE

Divorce could be the single worst thing that could happen to anybody both emotionally and financially.

It usually happens in the 40's and 50's due to the mid-life crisis or happens as soon as you are married i.e within the first 5 years.

When it happens within the first 5 years, it would be easy to come out of it as you would just have started to build a life for yourself. But if it happens in your late 40's or 50's, that is often the time when you would have built a solid financial base for yourself and have a strong relationship with your children. It would take a turn for the worse.

Even having a prenup would be of no use at times. During a divorce, your money is no longer yours to control. The state decides what to do with your money; how much of it goes where and who gets to see the children, when and for how long.

Divorce is when you realize even your children are not yours to see when you deem fit. Lives are destroyed when there is a divorce. People end up with their life savings wiped and all their pensions vanished.

It's the worst nightmare that could happen at the worst time. You will no longer have the strength to make that kind of money and will soon be rendered unfit to work.

What will you do then?

> "If the relationship can't survive the long term, why on earth would it be worth my time and energy for the short term?" — **Nicholas Sparks, The Last Song.**

Better build a strong relationship and nurture it. Stay with your partner for life.

Choosing a right partner with the right intentions is one of the most important prerequisites to start your journey towards financial freedom.

THE FINANCIAL CONVERSATION

Remember the girl who trusted me with £7000. I ended up marrying her. It was the best thing that ever happened to me.

By that time, I had disappointed her in money management so much that she had started managing her money for almost a year.

Now, I wanted to make sure that we had a single financial goal and plan after being motivated by reading the book "Think Big and Kick Ass" by Bill Zanker & Donald Trump. Except that, she would not agree to it. It was the most difficult conversation we have ever had. We had to set up ground rules.

What could be worse? We had all these conversations over the phone. I was in Spain and she was in India. We were engaged by then and were about to get married in three months.

It has been a year and a half after marriage. I have lived up to my expectations. It is a promise for a lifetime. Still, have a lifetime left to live up to my expectations. I am sure that I will fail again.

As long as we are on the same page, we can still crawl out of any dire financial situations together.

11

The Power of Dreaming!

It all starts with a dream to become successful in life. The dream has to be justified with a definiteness of purpose. The purpose then drives us to plan and to take action. Keep repeating the action with discipline and there you have it! A glimpse of the path to success.

Assuming you are dreaming to become successful in the field that you love, you would find it relatively easy to learn from your mistakes. Learning from the mistakes fine tunes your skills & improves it to an extent that you become more and more valuable day by day.

WHAT IF I AM REALLY COMFORTABLE WHERE I AM?

You should start attending seminars by Tony Robbins or Harv Eker. They have the habit of making you realize your false perceptions. They make you really uncomfortable and uncomfortable is what we want everybody to feel. That's when people start taking action and start moving forward in life towards success.

Feeling uncomfortable about your current situation is the best thing that could happen to you.

Answer the questions mentioned below to help you find your meaning and purpose in life:

1. If you knew you were going to die in one year from today, what would you do and how would you want to be remembered?
2. If you had to leave the house all day, everyday, 10 hours a day, where would you go and what would you do?
3. If you had all the money in the world, how would you spend your time?
4. How do you feel about your current job / business / studies and how do you see your future in the same industry?
5. What were you working on when you lost track of time?
6. What do I love doing that provides value to others?
7. What am I good at doing which provides value to others?
8. What does the world around you need solving?
9. Imagine you went into a time machine of some sort and is in an airport 5 years from now waiting for your flight, you can feel someone tapping your shoulder from behind, your face burst into a smile, it was your friend. He says "I thought it was you, it has been a long time". Since you have some time to kill, you go on talking to catch up with him. When he asks you "how is your life?" You say "it is truly amazing" and you mean it! What do you think should

happen in your life in the following five years that will make you go "freaking amazing life!"?

Answering all the questions mentioned above has the potential to unlock your purpose in life. Being honest with yourself is the only thing which you have to be aware of. You can also find the same PDF questionnaire from the link mentioned below:

https://readorb.com/wp-content/uploads/2018/08/Finding-Your-Meaning-and-Purpose-in-Life.pdf

HOW DO YOU BECOME SUCCESSFUL IN LIFE?

You have probably heard that you have to provide value. Value also means helping people solve a problem. It has to be in your area of expertise.

How do you find an opportunity to solve a problem? Chris Guillebeau, Author of "$100 startup" has some really good insights.

1. Inefficiency in the market can be compensated by your product/services.
2. The advent of new technology or opportunity. For example – Android and play store in the late 2000's.
3. Being efficient and talented in your area of expertise.
4. Providing customer with what they want and not what you think they want.

DOES PROVIDING VALUE MAKE YOU SUCCESSFUL?

No. It simply provides you with an opportunity to earn. To become successful, you should be the kind of person that people think about in order to resolve that problem. "Losing my virginity" by Richard Branson has some perfect suggestions.

1. Make a positive difference in people's life. Doing good for others without expecting anything in return at times is good for business.
2. Believe in your Ideas and be the best you could possibly be in business/personal life.
3. Have fun along the way to success and always look after your team.
4. Never give up.
5. **Active Listening** – Take notes when necessary and keep facing challenges.
6. **Hire Your Weaknesses** – Delegate and spend more time with your family. Always listen to your families opinions and then make your own decisions.
7. **Go Offline** – Turn Off your Laptop and iPhone before you engage with the world everyday. Embark on the journey of your life and experience it to the fullest.
8. **Communicate, Collaborate And Then Communicate More** – Always remember to convey the ideas in a simplistic term.
9. **Do What You Love** – surround yourself with people you love and people who love you.

THE REAL PRICE OF NOT DOING WHAT YOU LOVE

I vividly remember the first time when one of my colleagues introduced me to the website wishandfly.com - an interesting concept in which the traveler pays a set amount of money, in this case, €150 per traveler and the traveler does not know where he/she is traveling before 48 hours of the date of travel.

The moment, I laid my eyes on it. I knew it had a great potential in India and wanted to create a website for exactly this purpose. I was sure that it would be a great success. There began a journey of Surprisetours.in. It took me nearly 3 months to finish the website and that meant that I did not learn anything about personal finance during those three months.

What next? I am in Spain, trying to run a surprise tours travel agency in India. Will it work out? it might. That would mean that I have to be available over the phone, provide a valid address, register the business, start a business account and market the website.

Will I be a millionaire the next day? Nop. I was enthusiastic about the opportunity to create the website but gave up on it as it was practically not viable since I was in Spain. It would mean that I spend a fortune to set up and start the business and most likely hire people and manage them remotely.

I gave up on it after three months. The website is still live earning a total of 0 rupee for the past four months. Then, I diverted my attention back to readorb.com. It is the one thing which I am certain that I will get back to, no matter what. I have practically experienced it.

Readorb is what I love, without learning about personal finance, I am a failure in my personal life. It is too important to give up. While learning about personal finance, this is the way that I would like to give back to the community. The website and all of its contents are free.

What's the big deal in running a website right? It's hardly giving back to the community. Try to do the same as a part-time job while also learning about personal finance. The content has to be a quality one else people would never visit it. There are thousands of financial websites out there. The last website which could be a success is Readorb and I am aware of that. Every business has to have its own niche. Mine is a personal financial plan for millennials and I know it works. How? I am a millennial myself.

All the personal financial advice provided here are tried and tested. Only out of the experience. Paving a clear financial path and planning for it is half the job done. The other half is to actually execute the formulated plan.

So, I gave up on surprise tours and I am back on learning about personal finance. I love learning about personal finance and just because there was an opportunity in India regarding surprise tours does not mean that I will succeed in it. Unless I love the fact of running a travel agency and am passionate about it, I will never be a success. In fact, I will be a failure.

Lesson well learnt: **Do only what you love and do it consistently**.

Part Three

Income Management Strategy

12

Do You Really Need a Budget to Become Financially Free?

We all love freedom. Doesn't budgeting restrict our freedom of spending?

Yes, it does restrict our freedom to spend. That's the whole point but it will not feel that way when you get used to the budget.

The initial inertia required to start practicing to budget is minimal. But how many of them stick to the budget every month? What about one year? 10 years and your lifetime?

It's a habit which you should start to befriend rather than hate.

As it is the single habit which will definitely move you closer to your financial freedom.

Think of yourself as an organization with strict spending. Don't overspend it as you have other tasks to spend it on as well.

> "Start to control the money else it will start controlling what you do"

Freedom to spend the money when you want however you want comes with a price. Money begins to control your freedom.

Let's find out what I mean by that. Every individual has a finite amount of income that he pockets.

Majority of the individuals who do not like to budget their spending will eventually learn how to spend all their income before the month ends.

Just Google "famous stars being bankrupt", you will be bombarded with 647,000 results. Some of the most famous among them being **50 cents, Mike Tyson, Michael Jackson, Walt Disney** and **DONALD TRUMP!**

Many of them filed for bankruptcy due to various reasons. But it is not uncommon even among the most famous individuals.

If celebrities get bankrupt it is easy for them to revert back. But if you do it, it is going to be hard compared to the celebrities.

Better plan your expenditures and count your money before planning to spend.

GOING OVER THE BUDGET

Why do you want to plan to budget your expenses?

Is it because you are tired of not having money during the month end? Is it because you are unable to save for your next home?

Find out exactly why is it that you have decided to start budgeting.

For example, if you are tired of not having money during the month ends, how tired are you? Will you be able to stick to your budget for 90 days or more without taking a break?

It takes about 90 days for the habit to kick in. You have to be determined enough to pull it off.

> "The fact that you are losing something while not budgeting should be emotionally more painful than the joy of being able to spend."

If you do not have one or more pressing reasons to perform an act, you will give up some day or the other and end up living in a way you never intended to.

Even at the time when we truly intend to budget and start spending strictly on the budget, it is sometimes not possible to stick with it for various reasons.

Imagine a budget for one month with an income of $1,000.

Example –
1. Rent – $300
2. Utility – $100

3. Travel and food – $320

In the example mentioned above, it is easy to go over budget on the utility during winter due to electricity and gas usage.

It will indirectly result in your saving less in winter and more on summer due to utility charges.

Apart from that, you could have a restaurant budget / cheat- day budget.

You could come up with as many ideas as possible for adding something new and budgeting it.

While some of the budgets keep changing, others can reliably be static as the house rent, internet bill, transport expenses, and even food.

Strictly spend the food budget on food and utility on utility without excuses.

Always have a purpose for budgeting. Generally, the purpose of budgeting is to enable you to save/free up the money to invest.

Budgeting enables you to possibly prevent any financial blunders.

Taking a loan to speculate on the stock market because you don't have the habit of budgeting is a blunder.

If it is other people's money and if it comes with relative ease, we don't think twice before spending it.

"The pain of saving every little penny and watching it grow will make you think twice before you spend"

ALTERNATE WAY TO SPEND

There are others who choose to pay by card and generally find out that they have gone a little over budget this time.

We generally prefer to spend using the card as spending by cash and watching it dwindle is equally painful as saving the money one penny at a time and watching it go to waste.

Spend using cash, if you run out of money a week early every month. Try to plan a weekly budget.

Still thinking the budget is not for you? Even the governments run on budget. They plan for everything and even for the future. Why do you think you shouldn't?

LOSING THE PURPOSE TO BUDGET

Having truly experienced a real lack of money continuously for a few years, I had no option but to budget my expenses. I was frugal while working in India. I had no option but to be frugal.

My income would barely suffice for my day to day living. It was not much. I was in a lock-in period with the company in India. I was supposed to serve a compulsory two-year term for being trained in IT.

I honestly thought that I was financially doomed back in March 2015 when I signed the contract. I knew it was the right career move. Learned a new technology which was worth the risk which I took.

By April 2016, after my serving one year in the company, it had to shut down due to various financial reasons. I was jobless for one month, during which I applied for a job in Spain.

Luckily, I got the job and migrated to Spain. With the sudden surplus of money, I could spend every penny which I earned and no one could possibly blame me.

I never cooked for the first two months in Spain. I was by no means experiencing the same lack of money when I was in India. By all means, I was living a lavish life with the money that I had earned while also saving 70% of my salary.

Spending money never felt right even after earning enough to save 70% of my salary every month. Something told me to be frugal always. I still have the lack of ease to spend which was largely attributed to the series of events which I had previously mentioned.

But, there was a problem. I never had any purpose to save the money. Although I saved up 50% of the money for the marriage expenses, the remaining 20% was at my disposal. I could have spent them all.

Every month, I started saving the remaining 20% for no particular reason. Just out of habit. It was about €250 every month, It slowly grew. After marriage, the money had grown to a grand total of €2000.

During the 8 months alone in Spain, I read around 35 books, largely because I never had the internet and the summer was too hot to venture outside. The combined wisdom of these 35+ books taught me to save for the rainy day.

I decided the money which I was saving without any real purpose is an **emergency fund!**

It was a new term which I stumbled while reading Dave
Ramsey's book. Later in 2017, I had learned that women largely crave for financial security. Doesn't matter if they realize it or not.

There would be a general discomfort when you ask a woman to travel 8000km without any financial security. The emergency fund would then act as a security for my wife.

For some reason, she freaks out when the emergency fund runs dry! So, I always ensured a minimum emergency fund of €2000.

13

I Cannot Save a Penny More!

Why aren't people saving?

You'll start saving money when your future needs become more important than your current desires.

People spend on things which they do not need. One could easily avoid regular restaurant expenses by cooking from home. That's the reason why people are not saving. Your current needs outweigh the necessity to save more for tomorrow.

People often tend to see saving as cutting back on spending.

If you tend to be one of them, it's time to change the perspective. Else your subconscious mind will induce pain whenever you try to save more money. Why? Because you are putting off something. The pain should be replaced with pleasure. That's the only way you will start saving more money.

What are the ways to save more money if I cannot find a penny more to save?

CREATE A BUDGET

Create a budget, plan your budget and stick to it. Allocate money to your expenses like food, electricity & gas bill, home rent/mortgage, travel and miscellaneous expenses. Have a budget and allocate a percentage of your income towards all the categories and stick to the plan until the end of the month.

I am pretty sure the first time you try to create a budget some of the sectors will run out of money. Don't worry you will get better the next month.

"The trick to mastery is repetition"

The key to creating a new budget is to just start saving a $100 the first month or any amount you can afford for that matter and create a budget with the remaining amount. Stick to it until the end.

Still, can't find enough money to save? Can't find that extra $100?

LATTE FACTOR

Latte factor is the answer to your questions. Latte factor was first introduced by David Bach in his book "The Automatic Millionaire". We can all find our Latte factors in life.

All we have to do is write down all the expenses that we had for that day after reaching home. You will find that you grabbed a cup of coffee from Starbucks for $4 or that you have muffins for $4.75 everyday for your breakfast. Well, that is $80 for one month if you can choose an alternative plan to fetch that cup of coffee. Everybody has one. There is not a single soul who cannot find the one thing he is spending the extra money on.

Eating outside, drinking outside, the extra expense which we seduce ourselves with are all the excuses we make to spend the money today instead of saving them for our future.

BRING IN MORE MONEY

Are you the extraordinary person who does not have any Latte factor in your life? Or not willing to cut back your spending but choose to find an alternative approach to saving? Find new ways of bringing in more money to your family. It may be an extra part-time job every weekend that you have to do or a passive stream of income. Every penny you add extra will go towards the saving.

Find your savings. Plan for the future. Have a purpose to drive your income higher. Save more when you earn more.

CLEAR CUT STRATEGY

In the next chapter, we will be allocating a budget for you. This strategy is designed to pay yourself first. All the strategy mentioned in *Chapter 13: Income Allocation* is currently being practiced by myself.

I can personally assure you that this budgeting strategy is extremely efficient in paying yourself first. I recommend to have a separate account for your savings and have a separate account for your spending.

Transfer all the "Pay Yourself First" money automatically on the 1st of every month. Never fail to do that as the day you stop paying yourself first will be the day you have failed to live up to your dream.

Always! Have a "lavish spending" account which is used to fulfill your desires. This never fails to motivate you always to anticipate the next month.

Income allocation is by far the first strategy every individual has to implement in their lives. If you do not measure what comes in and decide what goes out and how, you will end up spending everything you earn.

Out of your savings account goes your debt repayments except for your mortgage. It is designed this way for a reason which we shall discuss in *Part Four: Debt Management Strategy*.

Your Emergency Fund and Your Savings account are one and the same. The Emergency Fund is deposited as Fixed Deposit in the Savings Account which you have allocated by "Paying Yourself First".

Your expenditure account will pay your rent/mortgage, insurance, self education expenses & charity expenses.

You will spend the food/travel expenses in cash. It will ensure that you always have money in your wallet and that will be a constant reminder of your habit of budgeting.

We will use the savings account later to invest periodically if necessary to attain your mid-term and long-term goals. So it is mandatory to have a savings account in order to begin implementing personal financial success habits.

Have you allocated a savings account? Alright! Let's move on!

14

Income Allocation Strategy

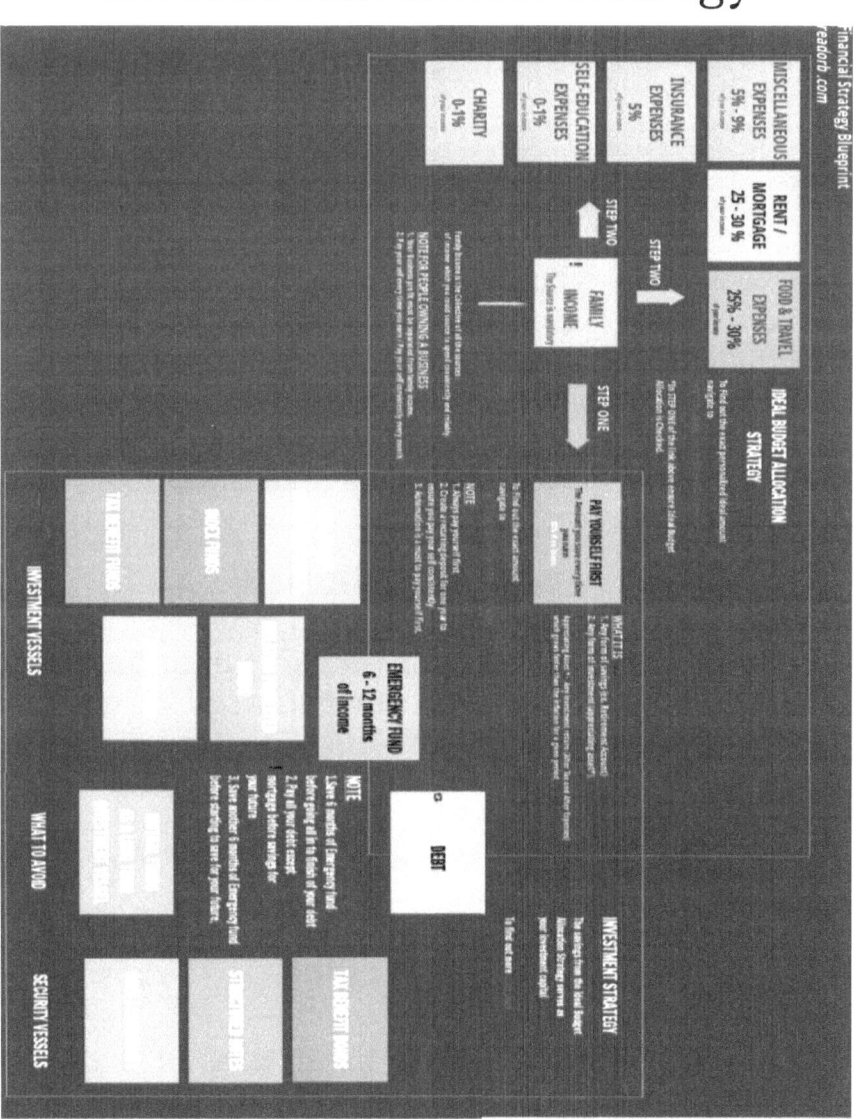

The income allocation blueprint is a suggestion to allocate a certain portion of your income.

Find the link below to navigate to the income allocation strategy blueprint mentioned above:

https://readorb.com/wp-content/uploads/2018/02/Financial-Strategy-Blueprint.png

This income allocation suggestion works really well when you include your partner as well. To prevent you from calculating all the budgeting allocation yourself, we have developed a tool to help you calculate it.

It is a free tool which could be used by anybody to help them find their ideal budget allocation.

WEALTH BUILDER

We have developed a tool for you to automatically calculate your income allocation strategy.

In order to calculate your wealth, Find the link below:

https://readorb.com/tools/wealth-builder/

It will navigate you to the wealth builder tool which loads in Dollars / Euros / Rupees.

This tool has the power to calculate all of the below mentioned expenses in this chapter and more.

To help you understand the strategy better, all of the components mentioned in the strategy is broken down and explained in bullet points.

Food / Travel Expenses

1. The food and travel expenses are set to 25 – 30%.
2. They include your groceries, everyday travel expenses.
3. As your income grows you could include your expenditure for hotel and holiday travels within the food and travel allowances.
4. Food / travel expenses are better **spent on cash**.

Emergency Fund

1. You don't need a credit card to cover your emergency expenses. That's what insurance and emergency funds are for!
2. Six months of your monthly income as an emergency fund is a must to even start your journey towards financial freedom.

Debt Repayment

Find this strategy in *Part Four : Debt Management Strategy*.

Miscellaneous Expenses

1. The miscellaneous expenses cover any expenses other than your food/travel,

rent/mortgage, insurance, self-education and charity expenses.
2. Miscellaneous expenses can be expended for anything which you desire.
3. The expenses might include your occasional visit to theatres / any pleasures that you find soothing to occasionally encounter.

Insurance Expenses

1. Insurance expenses are generally different from the "Pay Yourself First", as they are a form of security and also fall under expenses.
2. It is a security as it provides you the cover if things go bad but often they don't.
3. Your car insurance, life insurance, medical insurances and every other sort of insurance go in here.
4. If your insurance expenses are more than the allotted budget, maybe it is time to drop a handful of them or opt a reduced plan.

Self-Education Expenses

1. Often you can learn without spending a dime but there comes a time when you have to, if you need to have an in-depth knowledge of something, it will cost you.
2. Again, they are advisable only for those who could take care of their needs and afford to spend in this category.

Charity Expenses

1. The charity expenses are only for those who earn enough salary to take care of themselves.

Investment Strategy

Investment Vessels

1. They are the most reliable forms of investments for the long-term which appreciate more than the inflation.
2. Ensure that you check the quality of the investment vessel before investing.

For more information on individual investment vessels, please check the *Part Six: Investment Management Strategy*.

Security Vessel

1. They are the safest form of investments which protect the investor from the downslide and the disadvantage of a security vessel is the lower returns which it yields.
2. They are a must invest segment, you need a reliable money source to fall back on.
3. Annuity Plans are listed under investment but they are also a form of security.

Avoid Mutual Funds at all costs. Check out the book by Tony Robbins "Money - master the game" for over 600 pages advising why not to invest in a mutual fund.

WHAT'S WORSE?

Income allocation could be demanding at first. Honestly, what could be worse than managing your income?

Not managing your income!

What is the cost of not managing your income? Millions!

Let me tell you a real-life story of a man who inherited fifteen acres of land and two triple bedroom houses when he turned twenty-five.

Let's call him John. John lived with his mother when he inherited his father's wealth. By all means, John's father Jone was hardworking and a self-made millionaire. Jone had a medical condition induced by excessive cigarette smoking which ensured his premature death. Upon Jone's death, his three male children inherited all his wealth. That brings us to John.

John got married really early and inherited money from his father. He hardly had the necessity to learn about finance and has scarcely worked his entire life. He didn't really need to, as his inheritance would feed him and his family for a lifetime.

So, he never really worked his entire life. His wife was by all means extravagant. They both lived a really comfortable life and never really wanted to work. So, they would spend all their earnings from their cardamom estate. Any farmer would know to keep a portion of their earnings to reinvest on that property. Apparently, John didn't. He spent all their earnings from their real estate and borrowed money from a private lender to reinvest on the cardamom estate.

The private lender would charge 100% interest rate on the loan amount. We call them "Kandhu Vatti", meaning, private lending at a ridiculously high rate. They were known to borrow this money for personal extravagance as well.

Could anyone survive this? No, apparently they started selling their property to pay off their debts and were often known to keep a small portion of their "Kandhu Vatti" remaining. God knows why! I guess, they just wanted to spend all the money for themselves. That could be the only possible explanation.

To teach us to live a mindful life, my parents and relatives would quote "They once hired a car to travel". It was back in the 80's, when only the ultra-rich could afford a car and the poverty rate in India was close to 60%.

Slowly but steadily, they lost their wealth. John also had the habit of gambling. He once went to jail for gambling as gambling is banned in India. He would often drink like a fish. Now, John is worth a total of 0 rupees.

He is in his 70's and is a victim of a stroke. Stroke induced by stress. What could be worse right? Nope, he failed to educate his children and hence some of them are determined to abstain from work for their entire lives.

The last time I saw them was back in 2008 when they were living in their only home. I later found out that, they had sold that home and lent some of the money to a person whom they knew but they never got that back as well.

John's life is filled with tragedy. He now relies on his son who never intends to work.

If there is one thing which could have changed their life, it was personal finance and budgeting.

I also know enough tragedies to **conclude that any person who is willing to work hard at an early age with enough determination to succeed in life will build a strong financial base for him and his family to prosper.**

Part Four

Debt Management Strategy

15

Emergency Fund: Why is it Important?

Have you ever noticed that we donot keep staring at someone for no reason? It makes everyone uncomfortable.

We only do so when the emotions are strong enough and even then rarely consistently unless the other reciprocates.

Other 4 senses do not have this intimate interaction. Any other species which relies on smell or hearing does not have this intimate emotional interaction.

We as a species who rely on emotions to guide us on the right path should also be able to equally rely on the habits and characters.

Much of these habits and principles are nurtured in the childhood.

One among them is the necessity and willingness to save. If we do not find pleasure in doing so and if the emotion – pleasure, pain, insecurity is not strong enough, then it is hopeless to start saving money and trying to get your finances right.

You will find out that you are starting to save some money to get your finances right only to find out that you stopped doing it in the next few months.

> "We are what we see and experience in life.
> We cannot possibly be anything more"

If you have experienced poverty, misery, and powerlessness for an extended period of time, so much so that you hate to experience them ever again, you will start to get your finances straight.

What about those who have experienced the comfort and is used to being comfortable in life. They are usually the middle class, the major consumers of the society.

It is going to be hard to break that cycle of spending to be comfortable in life.

The starting point to breaking that cycle comes in the form of saving - saving for emergencies.

CREDIT CARDS

We all have credit cards, don't we? We generally use them for emergencies.

The whole point of saving the money for an emergency fund is to instill a sense of security and start funding your emergencies by yourself.

What's the whole point of saving and liberating yourself from consumerism if you find solace and comfort under the credit card which is also something that you consume?!

A credit card is a commodity that you are consuming and paying for it later.

If you have a 12-month emergency fund basket and are having multiple streams of income, will you really think of having credit cards in your life?

Credit cards are an abomination to rely on for emergencies.
They fund your emergencies (the money that you can't afford). If you can't afford it this month, how could you possibly repay the debt in the next few months?

What if there is another emergency the next month?

Emergencies are an eventuality in life. The emergency expenses that you have not predicted for this month will happen to every individual one day or the other.

Are you protected for emergencies with your savings?

Benefits of an Emergency Fund:

1. Protected by your money, the sense of security and ownership is strong.
2. You will be able to experience life with a feeling of security and strong positive emotions.

3. Could pave the way to take risks and experience life, thereby having a possibility of opening new streams of income.
4. Wanting to extend this security that you have experienced in finance to all aspects of your life and thus making you strive for excellence.

The first step to getting your finances right is to start with an emergency fund according to Dave Ramsey, the author of "The Total Money Makeover".

It makes complete sense as starting whatever else must not be hindered by unexpected financial burdens in your life.

It paves the way to finish the other endeavors rather than halting it until the emergency is sorted.

COMFORT ZONE

> "A comfort zone is a beautiful place but nothing grows there!"

We all have our comfort zones. It's a place where life just happens to move along with minimal effort from your end.

As beautiful as it may sound. There is no growth there because all the action is happening outside your comfort zone.

> "Action takes effort; effort has no place in the comfort zone"

Can you name all the famous people that you know? Why do you know them?

The simple answer is that you know them because of the work they do. They are nobody without their success in their work.

The work you do has to be yours and has to solve a problem and make life easy to live for others.

> "You should not just love your work but own it"

Do what you do, do it with love and passion for the work. Begin! Learn! Excel! Start to solve greater problems. You will face hurdles in life - financial, personal and professional. Learn to stay calm. One of the key things that are going to make your life easy is an Emergency Fund.

It paves the way to stop worrying about the next calamity and to start taking action. Do what you want to do in life. Experience true freedom!

A SERIES OF UNFORTUNATE EVENTS

Working abroad could be a life-changing experience for anyone. That proved to be true with the recent set of events which had unfolded during my stay in Spain.

Happy that I didn't have to fulfill my two-year mandatory work in India due to the sudden closure of the company in April 2016. I signed an unbreakable contract with another consultancy which renews every year in order to work in Spain.

So began my journey to Spain. I found the unbreakable contract to be a plus, as I want to settle down somewhere abroad, largely due to the difference in the lifestyle between India and other developed nations.

I was happily working till the start of March 2018 in Spain through the Indian company with an unbreakable contract. The visa was intercompany transfer visa. The Indian company has made a partnership with another consultancy in Spain. Let's call the Spanish consultancy "B". "B" then contracts me to a multinational company as a contractor.

Everybody was happy with this arrangement until "B" decided to sell the existing contract with the multinational company to "C" along with all the people working in it through "B".

What's wrong? Things quickly get complicated as the Indian company does not have any existing partnership with Spanish consultancy "C" which currently holds all the rights to contract me for that particular multinational company.

All the employees who came through the Indian company were thrown out one fine morning on the 9th of May 2018. We could no longer work for the multinational company.

We honestly thought we were fired! Until then, I knew no one from company "C" and thought that the Indian company or the consultancy "B" would come to the rescue.

No one turned out to care about what had happened and the only person who came to the rescue was consultancy "C". We were supposed to work remotely inside the consultancy "C" for the multinational company for a few months until our "situation" was sorted.

My wife was quick to find an opportunity in this dilemma. She requested me to ask consultancy "C" if they would hire me directly.

As luck would have it, it did not come to that before I could ask them. Consultancy "C" offered that exact scenario as an option to resolve this current "situation".

I was swift in letting them know my intention of joining the consultancy "C" directly. That would mean that I would be terminating my supposedly unbreakable contract with the Indian company.

I didn't give it much thought. The sum payable as per the contract was a staggering $50,000 which by no means is a small amount. I still signed a contract with the consultancy "C". Luckily, the contract would no longer be valid until the immigration approves the contract.

It was the first week of June 2018. The immigration authorities in Spain are notorious for their vacation during the summer. I was certain that it would take at least one month for the immigration to approve the contract.

Until then, I would be paid by the Indian company and the consultancy "B" through consultancy "C".

Everything was planned and everyone is happy, right? Nop. Apparently, the Indian company grew desperate and wanted me to renew the existing contract with them.

Honestly how do you expect me to renew the contract with the Indian company which no longer has the right to contract me for that particular multinational company?

It is to be noted that the Indian company in question does not have any other contract with other companies in Spain. The total strength of the Indian consultancy is a grand total of 11 people.

Wow! I informed the Indian company of my intentions to terminate the contract by the end of the contract period!

A series of unfortunate events unfolded:

1. I was forced to find a new home with a notice period of 3 days in a country whose language I barely speak, as the accommodation I stayed was from the consultancy "B".
2. Social Security payments from the consultancy "B" has stopped.

3. The salary payment from the Indian company for the last month in question (June 2018) was never received.
4. Experience letter along with the past three months payslips was never received.
5. I was blackmailed by the Indian company to sign the contract which I never did.
6. I was forced to shift my house while not being paid.
7. Seeing all the commotion, the multinational company stopped allowing us to work remotely and wanted us to join them after receiving a valid approval from immigration.

Jobless, homeless, unprotected by social security while being unpaid for a month in a country whose language I barely speak was an unbelievable experience. I used up half of my emergency fund.

Fortunately, my wife had found a job five months prior. So she had a steady stream of income in our family. Our visas are due to expire shortly.

What do you think would have unfolded if for some reason, my wife chose not to work and I had no emergency fund?

I would have signed another unbreakable contract with the Indian consultancy and would have let them suck me dry.

The consultancy "C" offered us 3 times more than what the Indian consultancy and the consultancy "B" had offered previously.

Such an opportunity was rare due to the visa & language constraints which I had. I would have easily let the opportunity to pass if I had no emergency fund.

The risk would have been too much. The reward would have to proportionately outweigh the risk. That was made possible by increasing the streams of income in our family and having saved a comfortable emergency fund as a cushion to absorb the negative impacts of risk.

I could comfortably say that **emergency funds allow you the space to choose what you would truly want, rather than be constrained by your circumstances.**

I truly experienced the freedom of choice due to our opting to choose to save for emergencies. I believe you can experience the same when you have a comfortable cushion for yourself.

16

Debt Analysis: Analysing Your Financial Past?

How much are you in debt? You need to analyze the past. If you are in debt make sure you do not stack up anymore. That's half the battle against debt won! The need to stop stalking up more debt has to come from within.

Knowledge of how the money work is the first step against personal debt. Check out the video from the link mentioned below to know the basic mechanics of how the money machine works as explained by Ray Dalio (*67th Richest Man in the world*). It is a short 30 minutes video which covers all the basics of global economics and it is a must learn.

https://readorb.com/how-the-economic-money-machine-works/

Become an insider and know the rules before you get in the game.

> "When I look into the future, it is so bright that it burns my eyes" – **Oprah Winfrey.**

Most people overestimate what they can do in a year and underestimate what they can achieve in a decade according to Tony Robbins from the book "Money - master the game".

Let's analyze the types of debt starting with a credit card.

> "You have to know the rules of the game and then play better than anyone else" – **Albert Einstein**.

CREDIT CARD DEBT

How many credit cards do you have? And how much do you owe to the credit card companies? Credit cards are meant to be short-term debts and it was never meant to be paid off over a year, God forbid for a decade. Do you know how much you are paying as an interest on that credit? It is close to 18%. That's 20 dollars for every 100 dollars you borrow.

Credit card companies flock to provide one for every person out there. They want you to buy something from credit card and hopefully not repay it immediately. If you do then you are not making any money for the credit card companies. This is often the first debt to repay.

EDUCATION LOAN

Young and In Debt – people who are in debt due to educational loan should aim for financial security by clearing off the loan. Education loan is the single largest loan repayment apart from the home loan for every individual out there. Most of them are in debt to their neck. The second loan that has to be repaid is the educational loan. There is a sense of freedom and achievement while repaying every loan that we ever took.

People take $40,000 in loan and choose to repay it for the next 15 years in installments. Have you ever calculated how much are you paying by the end of the repayment tenure? It will cost 2 to 2 and half times the original amount if the loan is taken over 15 years or more.

Indian banks provide an opportunity to borrow for a period of 15 years while starting your repayment after you complete your studies without any cap but needs a collateral to be submitted.

For education loans provided within the country, the maximum amount of 7.5 lakhs can be provided with security for a period of 8 years of repayment with a gestation period of 6 years.

For example, If you borrow 4 lakh rupees without any security as an educational loan and start repaying them after the five year gestation period with an interest rate of 12% per annum (P.A), you would be paying double the amount borrowed by the end of the repayment tenure.

HOME LOAN

Your financial planner, real estate agent and accountant all call your house an asset. But in reality, it is a liability according to the book titled "Rich Dad Poor Dad" by Robert Kiyosaki. Although I would choose to say it is a security and not a liability. He takes a very simple approach. Anything that puts money in your pocket is an asset and anything that takes money away from your pocket is a liability.

He also says that if you choose to rent your home to tenants and loose money it's a liability. That's only if the money you take from the tenants is less than the money you repay to the banks for the home loan.

If you haven't paid for the home in full and have a loan for the home, it is an asset for the bank and a liability for you according to the book. Although the thought is extreme you can choose to take it as a security. Your home is in the security bucket.

CAR LOAN

> "Bad debt is a debt that makes you poor such as credit card debt, car loans, and more. This is the type of debt used to buy liabilities" – **Robert Kiyosaki.**

If there is absolutely one thing that you shouldn't take a loan to buy, it is a car. The car is our one deadly commodity that loses value the minute you drive it outside the store. Most cars lose 30% of the initial value but it could be more depending on the demand or the lack of it.

Second-hand cars are always the best choice if you ask me as the second hands do not lose a lot of value when you choose to sell them. Everybody changes their car at least once in his or her lifetime. The average lifetime of a car at the maximum is 250,000 miles. Keep that in mind the next time you buy a car.

What is your financial position? How much have you borrowed so far? How long will it take before you repay the loan? What is the percentage of income that goes to your loan repayment after taxes? Remember you are choosing to spend your future income today by borrowing.

17

Debt Management Strategy

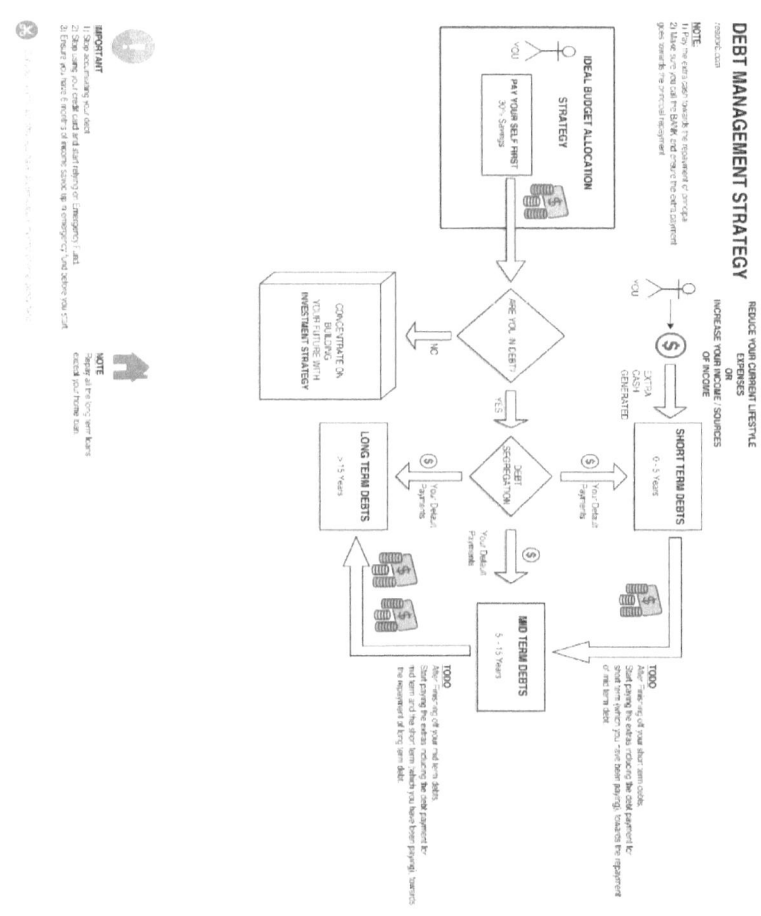

Debt management requires your utmost commitment to get rid of debt. The first step in making sure that you start reducing your debt is an emergency fund.

Find the below mentioned link to download the debt management blueprint:

https://readorb.com/wp-content/uploads/2018/02/DEBT-MANAGEMENT-BLUEPRINT.pdf

You need to accumulate six months of your income as an emergency fund before venturing into debt repayments. You do not know what is going to happen the next month.

Make sure that you are covered for your emergencies. After you have 6 months of your emergency fund accumulated, cut your credit card. You do not need them.

All the excuses for having a credit card is to cover for emergencies. Stop accumulating more debts.

Saving 30% of your salary as emergency fund will take you 18 months to accumulate the 6 months income as an emergency fund. So, start saving soon.

Find 30% of your income. Start earning more money by opening up multiple streams of income. Just find them! Always pay your default debt payments.

I realize that you are in debt because of the lack of money. If you want to break this cycle, you need to find more money / save more money by cutting down your expenses. That's the only way out.

Start taking control of your finances. Anyone in debt is either earning too little or spending too much. Which category are you in?

Spend only the bare minimum towards food, travel, school fees, insurance, debt repayments, house rent and save the rest.

If you cannot afford to have kids, don't have them till you increase your income.

If you are like me, saving 6 months of your income as emergency fund will give you a sense of security. A deep satisfaction for starters.

Use that to repay all your debts. Start by segregating all the debts in terms of how long it takes for you to repay.

1. Short Term Debt is any debt which is paid within the next 5 years.
2. Mid Term Debt is repaid within 5 - 15 years from today.
3. Long term Debt is any debt which takes more than 15 years to repay.

Now, where does your 30% of savings go after accumulating 6 months of your income as an emergency fund?

1. Pay your short term debt first. They are the debts for which you pay maximum interest rates. Finish it off ASAP.

Now, after finishing off your short term debts, you must have liberated more cash. I.e. Your cash which you were repaying your short term debt + 30% of your income.

1. Use this cash flow to repay your mid term debts. Finish them off.

Now, after finishing off your mid term debts, you must have a better cash flow than ever before. Your short term debts payments which you were repaying + your mid term debt payments which you were paying + 30% of your income.

1. Use this cash flow to repay all of your long term debts except your home mortgage.

Make sure that you call your bank every single time you are repaying extra to ensure that the extra cash goes into the principal repayment.

Certain banks have the unhealthy practice of not doing that. It is better to always ensure this and if you hold a debt and want to reduce the interest charged, some countries have the option to transfer all the debt to another company which offers to provide lesser interest rates.

If your country has that option, make sure that you make the most use of this option. Call your credit card company to ensure that they reduce your interests on the debt or you want to move all your debts to another company which has a reduced interest rate for your credit card loan.

All the developed nations have the option to transfer all your credit card balance to another credit card company at 0% interest rates. Make sure, you do not stack more debts as they will be charged at a standard rate rather than 0%.

This option of credit card balance transfer is available in India as well. There is a restraint though. You need to stay in one credit card company for at least a year before you can transfer your credit card debts and the credit card balance transfer is particularly beneficial if you find a bank which is willing to take the credit balance at 0%.

So, after repaying all of your debts. Make sure that you invest your new cash flow into your investment strategy. This strategy could take you anywhere between 6 months to about 10 years to repay all of your debts.

The repayment period highly depends on how deep are you in debt.

For example, if you only have credit card debts, you could easily repay them by first transferring all your debt to a 0% interest account and repaying the credit balance ASAP.

18

Credit Cards: How to Increase Your Credit Score

Before reading Ramit Sethi's book – "I Will Teach You To Be Rich", I thought there are only two ways to finance your budget - cash or debit card.

> "Getting started is more important than becoming an expert" – **Ramit Sethi.**

Never imagined a scenario where people are paying for their food with a credit card but that could be a good thing if you are disciplined enough.

There is a third way – Paying using credit card according to Ramit Sethi and I completely agree.

In all the developed nations, credit cards are most widely used. Majority of the financial advisers will want you to cut your credit card and throw it away.

We know the disadvantages of using a credit card.

1. Highest Interest Rates – 18% annually.
2. Fuels unnecessary consumption.
3. Buying the things you cannot afford.

But there are advantages of using a Credit Card as well.

1. Build a Credit Score (Example – FICO).
2. Flight and Hotel points on Credit Card.

To take advantage of these aspects of the credit card benefits one has to be extremely disciplined to only spend the money which you can repay the same month in full.

When you repay everything you borrowed using your credit card the same month or during the start of the next month, you will essentially wipe out any possibility of charging you for the money borrowed.

Credit card companies charge you on a per month basis. It is the worst mistake of your life if you have a credit card with debt racked up which you could never imagine to repay in the next few years.

Never pay the minimum on your credit card. Pay as much as you can and finish off the debt.

"Debt is bad; Credit Card is not."

Just like the quote "Money is only a means to an end", credit card is also a means to an end.

DO I NEED A CREDIT CARD?

In the developed nations where credit scores play a more important role in the economy to facilitate a car loan, yes but only for those who want to build a credit score to get a loan for buying a financial security or to invest and make more money.

If you really love the concept of loyalty points and flight points, spending with your credit card is the way to go.

If you are disciplined enough to repay your credit card debts on time every month, maybe it is not a bad idea to have a credit card but my advice would be to stick with just one.

Usually, one credit card is more than enough to build your credit score, flight point & hotel points.

DANGER!

Honestly, Beware of the dangers of being addicted to spending on credit card. It's a trap to lure you into getting a credit card.

The credit card companies all know that the majority of the people who get a credit card want to pay them on time and get it with all the right intentions to pay them on time but they eventually end up paying late.

Beware of the late payment fees. They are usually high, unexpected and will hit you hard.

Late payment fees are bad enough. What if you keep paying late and keep paying the minimum on the credit card and eventually max out your credit card?

When we get used to credit cards that's when we start taking it a little bit for granted and start paying a little late, start buying unnecessary consumables and buying things that you really can't afford.

To prevent that from happening, always remember to have a clear budget on the credit card. Have the money in your bank account and spend the allocated equivalent amount on your credit card.

You could spend all your food budget on the credit card and repay the entire amount on the day you pay your credit card bills.

That would be the perfect scenario but just like using a debit card for budgeting, the disadvantage remains the same.

We cannot stick precisely to the budget while paying by card.

Imagine you set $100 to spend per week on food and groceries. If you pay by card, at first, we borrow from the next week's budget then we slowly start to borrow from the next month's budget.

Then we will no longer be able to pay for food and groceries with the allotted budget as it will always be less than what you actually spend.

If it is a debit card you will not be able to spend the money if you do not have money. But if it is a credit card you will be able to borrow money at a ridiculous rate of 18% per year.

The best form of payment for keeping your budget is CASH.

CASH IS STILL THE KING!

If a credit card is a bad tool to be used for spending on budget and repaying the borrowed amount immediately, then we are talking about having no credit score.

If one does not have any credit score then you will not be granted any loan or probably a minimum loan amount.

But you only need a credit score if you are planning to be in debt for something in the near or far future.

Flight points and hotel points may seem appealing to everyone, especially when it comes for free but the danger of using a credit card still remains. It is important to treat credit card with respect as it is as dangerous and addictive as it is attractive.

You can give up on ever having a credit score and wanting to earn flight points and hotel points. That's the best course of action for the feeble heart.

If you are in a developing nation and the concept of credit score and earning loyalty points, reward points are nonexistent then forget about owning a credit card. There are better ways to live than to own a credit card.

19

Home Loan: Is it a Boon in Disguise?

It all starts with a dream of having a roof on top of one's head for the sake of their family.

But many end up not being able to afford to buy a home with cash.

Liberate your income by stepping down the expenses or stepping up your salary. Start saving a substantial portion of your salary towards owning a home.

Even if you want to buy a home with a mortgage/loan you might need to pay 10 – 30% upfront with your saved income.

Let's do some maths.

$100,000 home requires a minimum capital of $30,000 to be eligible to buy a home. By saving $1000 every month it would take 2 and a half years.

$30,000 / $1000 = 30 months / 2 and a half years.

$30,000 / $500 = 60 months / 5 years.

Let's do the math for the saving all the money $100,000

$100,000 / $1000 = 100$ months or 8 years and 4 months.

$100,000 / $500 = 200$ months or 16 years and 8 months.

The trick is to get the amount of money that you are planning to save right. You don't want to save too little every month and keep saving for 16 years and 8 months in a row only to find out that the home you would like to buy is no longer available for $100,000 but for $300,000.

SETTING A REALISTIC GOAL

1. What is the inflation rate of your currency? Is it 5%, 2% 10%?
2. What is the average rate at which the housing market inflates in your region?
3. What is your average savings allotted for building your new home?
4. What is the current average price of building a home of your liking in the area along with the land price?
5. How long is it going to take for you to save up the stipulated money to build a new home?
6. Will getting a home loan offset the housing inflation?

The thing to remember when obtaining a home loan is that you are willing to bet that the money that you will be paying for the home (along with the interest) will be less than the value of the home in 10 years, 15 years or 20 years.

But if you save up 30% of your house value while continuing to pay rent for your accommodation does it make sense? Or is it better to get the home loan instead?

From a purely mathematical standpoint,

Saving $1000 every month for 8 years and 4 months to reach $100,000 makes sense if the rent and the housing inflation stay just right while the money you put away earns you the right interest.

During these 8 years, you will also be spending around $50,000 on housing alone assuming that the rent is $500.

Let's say that the interest earned from the money saved every month through minimal risk funds are at an average of 8% compounded annually (*current interest rate on fixed deposit hovers around 7.1% P.A. as of 2018*).

Year	Cumulative Recurring Deposits Per Year	Total Interest Earned	Balance
1	Rs.12,000	Rs.593	Rs.12,593

2	Rs.12,000	Rs.2,195	Rs.26,195
3	Rs.12,000	Rs.4,884	Rs.40,884
4	Rs.12,000	Rs.8,749	Rs.56,749
5	Rs.12,000	Rs.13,883	Rs.73,883
6	Rs.12,000	Rs.20,387	Rs.92,387
7	Rs.12,000	Rs.28,372	Rs.112,372
8	Rs.12,000	Rs.37,956	Rs.133,956

In this case, It does not make sense to save up all the money while paying the rent for your housing. It is better to save the minimum on the housing and then buy your home ASAP.

Also, check the current house price trend. Every government has its own housing price index. India has its own relatively new Residex to track the current housing price trends in 50 different cities.

These indexes can be of great use to help you decide if it is the right time to buy a home in the area which you would like to. Some websites even have the option to choose year and price per square foot or square meter in the graph to accurately predict the price movement.

The major trend for the majority of the regions in India is downwards according to the Residex in 2017 (Residex is a National Housing Bank run housing price index for India and it calculates the housing price fluctuations in most of the cities in India) so it would be the right move to buy a property in the coming years in India.

Million Dollar Question!

If the house price trend is downwards or just rebounding from the bottom trough should you buy a property in the region if you have saved up the minimum capital of 20 -30% of the total estimated value of the house.

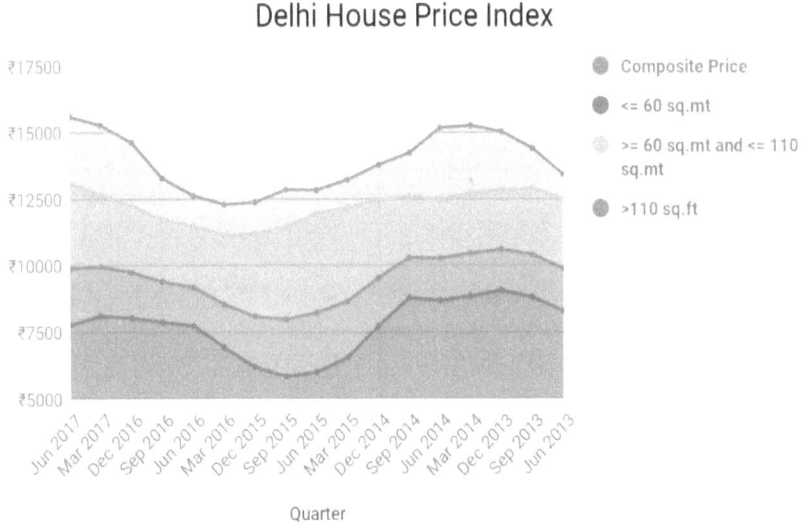

You could buy your home with a mortgage in Delhi for example during 2015 – 2016 as housing price were in its trough.

If we are planning to buy a home with about 1200 Square feet, the price per square feet is 12,859 rupees in September of 2015. We would need about 15,430,800 or 15.43 million rupees.

If we buy the same piece of property in June of 2017, the price per square feet is 15,605 rupees. We would need 18,726,000 or 18.72 million rupees.

Quarter	<= 60 sq.mt	>= 60 sq.mt and <= 110 sq.mt	>110 sq.ft
Jun 2013	Rs.8303	Rs.12,499	Rs.13,423
Sep 2013	Rs.8814	Rs.12,911	Rs.14,410
Dec 2013	Rs.9077	Rs.12,856	Rs.15,039
Mar 2014	Rs.8855	Rs.12,745	Rs.15,261
Jun 2014	Rs.8693	Rs.12,492	Rs.15,175
Sep 2014	Rs.8793	Rs.12,610	Rs.14,238
Dec 2014	Rs.7733	Rs.12,458	Rs.13,791
Mar 2015	Rs.6551	Rs.12,187	Rs.13,233
Jun 2015	Rs.6004	Rs.11,981	Rs.12,849
Sep 2015	Rs.5843	Rs.11,462	Rs.12,859
Dec 2015	Rs.6201	Rs.11,209	Rs.12,382
Mar 2016	Rs.6932	Rs.11,158	Rs.12,308
Jun 2016	Rs.7747	Rs.11,507	Rs.12,638

Sep 2016	Rs.7880	Rs.11,738	Rs.13,289
Dec 2016	Rs.8045	Rs.12,258	Rs.14,625
Mar 2017	Rs.8116	Rs.12,670	Rs.15,287
Jun 2017	Rs.7778	Rs.13,126	Rs.15,605

If you are in 2015 and all you see is the price dropping, you might wait for it to drop further only to find that it is starting to rise again.

The trick is to buy the property around the time frame between late 2015 – 2016. I understand it is hard to get it just right.

Opportunities arise when there is blood on the streets! When there is peak pessimism.

But between 2007 to 2012 the housing prices doubled and it has almost stayed the same for the next 6 years. So the long-term prospects of hurrying to buy a home today are questionable. If you buy a home today for 18.72 Million Rupees, the home price might stay the same for the next few years before moving up or down.

Chances are the house price will double during the 7 – 10 years of boom and drop significantly, then stay roughly in the same region for the following decade.

Chances are the house prices will double 2- 4 times during your lifetime. The trick is to never buy the property when it is at its peak and never try to sell the property when the price is in its trough.

CAN YOU GET IT RIGHT?

Yes, you can, you need more information on the history of the land prices in the region. Wait for the right opportunity and grab it when the time is right and pessimism is at its peak to get the best deal out of the housing market.

HOME LOAN

The question then arises - should you save all the money and buy a home with cash or save about 20 – 30% of the total value and buy a home today?

Let's say that you have put $30,000 upfront and took a loan for $70,000 from the bank.

Chances are you will be paying 1 and a half times to 2 and half times the total loan value if you are paying your home loan for 25 years.

The house price might only have doubled once during the time frame.

How to calculate if it's worth taking a mortgage now?

1. Calculate the total interest payment for the bank loan obtained.
2. Calculate the average home price you would like to pay today.
3. Calculate the home rent you would likely pay while saving to buy a home.

Let's check the difference between taking a mortgage and saving the money for buying a home using cash

1. (Total payment for the bank loan obtained along with interest payments + Your Initial upfront payment for your home)
2. (Average home price you would like to pay today + Compound interest earned while saving the money)-(Total Home Rent to pay during the period)

House price in the next decade or two can only be speculated but the general 2 – 5 year trend can be reliably predicted to either move upward or downwards and we also know that the house price is going to double at least once depending on the country in 25 years on an average.

These numbers should provide you with enough information to take appropriate action.

1. If the (Total payment for the bank loan obtained along with interest payments + Your Initial upfront payment for your home) is lesser, it makes sense to take a home loan.
2. If the (Average home price you would like to pay today + Compound interest earned while saving the money)-(Total Home Rent to pay during the period) is lesser, it makes sense to save the money with cash.

Since we have not taken the housing inflation for both the cases, the result should roughly provide the right answer.

RULE OF THUMB

1. If it takes less than a decade to save up the required capital and you predict the house price trend to be downward for the next 2-6 year period, SAVE THE MONEY TO BUY A HOME. When the trend starts to change and the price starts to spike up, you can consider buying a home with 50-60% down payment and repay the loan in less than a decade.
2. If it takes more than 15 years to save the money, may be consider stepping down and buying a 1 bedroom flat instead of a 2 bedroom villa.
3. After analyzing your house price index and if you are fairly certain that the prices are about to rebound from the trough soon and if you don't have 100% cash for buying your home and if you are certain that you would repay the home loan in the next decade, get the loan and buy your home.
4. If the home prices are stable for the past few years, it is better to keep saving the money and wait for the trough or signs of prices rising. Keep saving till then.
5. If you do not have any money saved up and you see there is a spike in the residential market or there is going to be a spike in the market, it's better that you let this opportunity pass. Be prepared for the next opportunity.

All the above scenario work well when the rent for the living is not more than 30% of your total income.

HOUSING BUBBLE

What happens if your country has a 3% down payment option to obtain a mortgage?

It is a great option. Go for it!

For example in the US, Fannie Mae currently offers 97% of the house value as a mortgage for a primary residence property with a loan not exceeding $453,100. The debtor should have a minimum credit score of 620.

Should you really save up 30% of your income before buying a home?

No! Definitely not.

Let's assume that you are buying a home worth $200,000. The minimum required down payment would then be $6000 which means that you will be taking a mortgage of $194,000.

That is a considerable mortgage which attracts an average compound interest of 4.6%.

Even if you choose to pay the mortgage in 360 installments which is a 30 year period, you would be paying around $1358 on a monthly basis which is substantial for an average person earning about $30,000 a year.

You would have paid around **$468,841.66** for a 30 year period.

How does it make sense to get a 3% down payment option then?

Let's look at the bigger picture.

1. From the lenders perspective, 3% down payment option is riskier.
2. From a government's perspective, they are too desperate to induce artificial growth.

Any rational person will know that if a person cannot possibly save 30% of the house value, he cannot pay off the house.

For a government to provide such a radical scheme, they must be really desperate for growth.

After introducing a 3% option for buying a home, anybody who cannot afford to save 30% of the total value of the home (which is the case with 37% of the families in the US) will start to go for the 3% option.

There will be a sudden spike in the housing market. All the people who couldn't previously afford to buy a home are now eligible to buy one with not much commitment at all. They are only paying 3% of the total value of a home.

That's not much of a ownership, the bank practically owns the home. The only belief is that the debtor will repay the mortgage on a monthly basis.

The sudden spike in the housing price will induce urgency and more and more people will start buying a home. So, if there is a 3% option, the best way is to get a new home with a 3% down payment.

What next? All the bad debtors will start defaulting on the payment. If enough people default on the mortgage then it will be a successful recreation of the 2008 housing bubble.

But that was due to subprime mortgages right? They typically had a credit score of less than 640.

Just like 2007, if people start buying more than one home what happens? It will be an eventuality that someone will default on the payment.

Whenever banks take the fall, the government will back them up with our tax dollars. This will be an eventuality.

What can you do about it? Take maximum advantage of the situation. When the media starts promoting people to buy a new home, start selling yours.

Chances are that you can sell yours at a much higher price. After selling yours and repaying all the mortgage left, you can invest the money on government bonds or any risk-free investments.

What if you do not sell the house but instead choose to keep paying the mortgage? When the house price hits rock bottom, you will essentially be paying a higher mortgage for a home which isn't worth as much.

It is generally painful and you would be lucky if your company was still afloat after the stock crash. Generally, the smaller companies take a harder hit.

The larger companies are generally backed by the governments. They have nothing to lose. Fire a few employees and get the balance sheet in order.

Anything can happen. I am not proposing a doomsday theory here. If you find an opportunity, it is always better to cash in on the opportunity.

After the fall, when no one wants to buy a home, go buy two of 'em.

Part Five

Savings Management Strategy

20

Savings Management Strategy

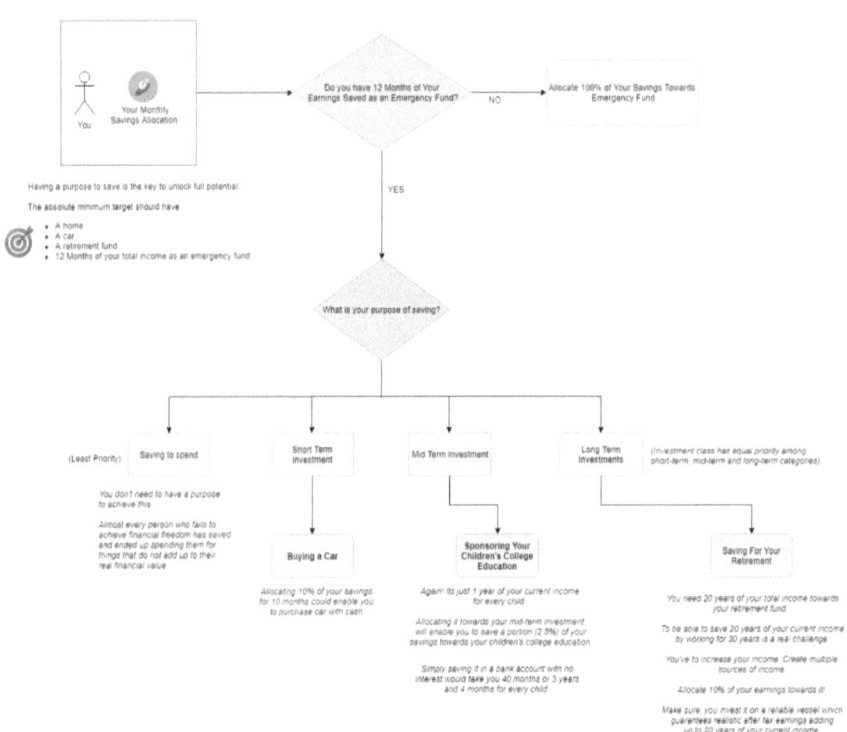

Savings management strategy is by far the simplest yet hard to implement amongst all the strategies. It demands that you change your mentality and destroy the previously held notions of money.

Find the link to the above mentioned savings management strategy below:

https://readorb.com/wp-content/uploads/2018/05/Savings-Strategy-Blueprint.png

It is like executing a demonetization if necessary to your own personal finance. Remove all the money held in the wrong hands and put it back to where the money originally belongs!

The habit of being frugal has to be developed in the place of lavish spending.

The savings strategy is simple. Check if you have 12 months of your monthly income as savings. If not, continue to invest all of your savings to repopulate your emergency fund.

Segregate your savings into four different strategies.

1. Savings to spend
2. Short-Term Investment
3. Mid-Term Investment
4. Long-Term Investment

You need to evaluate what you really want to be in life, not today but in the future. It demands that you know what you are doing now and where you financially are. Without a clear purpose for your money, you are bound to fail miserably.

As mentioned, you also need a strong emotion to back your purpose.

SAVING TO SPEND

The least preferable mode of saving compared to others. If you would like to buy an iPhone X for example, this is the bucket you are looking for.

All the expenses in this budget have to be reduced as much as possible. Do you really need an iPhone X? Can you settle for an iPhone 6 and would it serve the emotional purpose you are looking for?

Most people buy an iPhone for prestige and the respect. Can you make sure that the iPhone is not stolen? Do your friends have the same phone? Do they feel jealous of you?

My girlfriend was traveling from Mumbai to Kochi when the security inspection officer took her iPhone 6 (gold) to have a look. Nobody does that at the airport. It clearly signifies his intent. He likes it and would like to have it. I was not there myself as I was traveling to Chennai from Mumbai.

She forced the security inspection officer to return the phone by simply not allowing other passengers to pass her. She had to shout at the security officer to get it back. Yes! Actually, shout at them. When the passengers asked what happened, she conveyed the situation to other passengers and hence the security inspection officer returned the mobile back to my girlfriend.

How many of your friends are visibly greedy about other people's possessions?

SHORT TERM INVESTMENT

Short-term investment vessel includes your car as well. A car is a depreciating asset but you could put the money in a fixed deposit till you accumulate an adequate amount in order to buy a car. The last thing which you should be doing is to buy a car on a loan.

Save your allocated budget as a recurring deposit if you are in India or in a fixed deposit. Keep it safe and risk-free.

Short-term investment vessels are generally very risky. For example, Bitcoin investment in the wake of 2017. Bitcoins' stocks soared from $1000 by more than 1300% to $14,500 by the end of the year.

What happened the next year? It is hovering somewhere in the $6900 range now.

Short-term investments are risky! There is no doubt about it.

Stock market investments are meant to be for long-term for a normal investor like you and me.

Any short-term gamble might take a turn for the worse and you may not even know until after it hits you.

So better stick with fixed deposits, recurring deposits, and any risk-free low-interest investment vessels.

MIDTERM INVESTMENTS

A mid-term investment could be for your children's college education or any obligation which you can foresee 15 years ahead.

Be covered for such an event; they are going to graduate no matter what. Graduation is the minimum requirement nowadays and educational expenses are soaring year by year.

Do not let your children accumulate debt for education. It is the one essential thing in life which you could sponsor.

A mid-term investment vessel in India could be a PPF. A public provident fund offers an attractive interest rate of 7.6% and all the income deposited in it is tax-free. You could deposit a maximum of 150,000 rupees into your PPF fund. There could be a maximum of 1 PPF account for a working individual.

Other mid-term options include bonds, structured notes, annuity plans, real estate investment trusts, individual stocks and index funds.

Based on your risk tolerance, you could choose one investment and periodically invest in that particular fund.

LONG-TERM INVESTMENTS

The long-term investment must include your retirement. It is a must-have!

You are not going to be able to work one day or the other. You need to be covered for that. If you are procrastinating, think about the after retirement days where you have to rely on your children's ability to sponsor your livelihood, forcing them to pay for your medical expenses and having to rely on their income to buy medicine which could determine if you live a pain-free life.

Every part of your body might ache and you would no longer have the energy and mobility to earn as you did when you were in your 20's.

This should motivate you to keep saving no matter what for your retirement. Later, we will discuss how time plays a role in your retirement lifestyle.

If you choose to invest early for your retirement it could make a difference between retiring & not reducing your lifestyle and retiring & reducing your lifestyle to a bare minimum.

Generally, India has Employee Provident Fund(EPF) which serves as a retirement pension for employees.

All the income deposited in the EPF is tax-free and grows at a steady rate. The amount could be withdrawn after retirement, or in the event of a sudden death of the EPF account holder and a part of the money can be withdrawn for marriage expenses as well.

Other ideal long-term investment vessels include index funds, tax savings bond, real estate investments, structured notes and annuity plans.

All the savings strategy always has a purpose right? - Buying a car, saving for your retirement or sponsoring your children's education. Why is that? Other personal financial books speak about asset allocation without touching these aspects of your everyday life.

Are they complete? When I say allocate a 30% of your savings to fixed deposit, another 30% to Index Fund (VFINX) through a non-taxable account such as Roth IRA in the US / directly to EPF in India while making sure that the last 40% of your savings should be split as 30% and 10% in which 30% goes towards government inflation protected bonds and the last 10% should be invested in the purchase of stocks which deals with commodity/gold.

Does it sound appealing to you? It does not to me. Asset allocation based on the investment vessel lacks emotion. It is for the ultra-rich who choose to balance the risk vs reward. It means nothing to us.

All of the above mentioned stocks have to be purchased using the dollar cost averaging strategy.

You put in a set amount of money every month into the purchase of the stock. We have to use the power of compounding to our advantage. Slowly, but steadily our investments would rise, giving it a strong meaning and purpose like retirement savings, emergency savings and home purchase fund will provide you with a strong reason to keep pushing yourself to save more, earn more and invest more as the first million is the hardest.

THE FRIEND WHO LOST HIS LIFETIME SAVINGS

Remember my friend who outsourced his personal finance to his uncle? Let's continue talking about him.

He seemed a bit motivated about buying a home for himself. I do not know where he got the motivation from. Being curious about his financial situation, I asked him how he is willing to buy it and will he be taking a home loan.

He told me that his family had a life savings of 3,000,000 rupees in a fixed deposit and that he and his family are willing to utilize two third of the money plus another 1,000,000 rupees which my friend had saved up after working in Spain.

I was really happy for him. We left the conversation hanging and I thought he was looking for a good property for sale. After a few months, we were having a pretty deep conversation about his personal financial situation. It was about 6 hours long during which he revealed that his family's life savings of 3,000,000 rupees was handed over to his uncle for safe keeping. A fixed deposit was jointly opened to save the 3,000,000 rupees. The joint account holders were his uncle and his mother.

The handling of the account was left to the wills and fancies of his uncle.

His uncle had informed my friend of his act of taking an overdraft from the fixed deposit for about 1,200,000 rupees and that he intended to repay the amount in a few months.

My friends' mother was fully aware that the fixed deposit was expiring by May 2018, after which his mother promptly requested for the money back. He somehow convinced his mother of his intentions to repay the money in the coming few months and in fact, he had withdrawn 1,800,000 rupees.

When they asked for the remaining amount to be repaid, he had no intention to repay the remaining 1,200,000 rupees and is intentionally postponing the repayment. Once his mother had forced an answer from his uncle he replied: "Let me remortgage my only home and go to the streets. But don't worry; I shall repay the amount with the mortgage".

I have to say at this point that his uncle was of much help to my friends family when they needed it most. He had sponsored four years of his high school education and his sister's education. He also sponsored an operation for his mother and honestly my friends family had no money to pay for the operation back then. All these would financially account for about 500,000 rupees.

I convinced my friend that his uncle had utilized all the money for sure and he had no intention of repaying the money back.

I also remember that his uncle wanted my friend to invest in Bitcoins in the wake of the new year 2018 and I promptly informed my friend not to as it would prove to be a dire mistake.

He also informed me that his uncle is investing in bitcoins because he thinks it is the hot new investment. During this six hours of conversation which we had recently, he said: "the bitcoin investment which my uncle made was a loss, A total loss of 500,000 rupees and all the money used to invest was from my family's fixed deposit".

"Wow" was the word which came to my mind. He continued "He also took all of my mother's gold. All 30 sovereigns of it including my mother's thali and it was five years ago. He still did not return an ounce of gold which he borrowed ".

Thali is the equivalent of a wedding ring in European countries. The validity of the marriage is stored in the form of a symbol "Thali" and the emotions around it are so strong.

For a married woman to donate it for the sake of his brother is a true act of love & trust.

That was all of their families wealth. Everything! They live in a rented apartment in the town and his father earns just enough to cover all their families expenses. His mother, being frustrated as she is, kept asking his brother for at least the thali. So far! No luck.

Just recently, his mother started asking my friend to buy a thali for her. He was in the hope that his brother might return the thali back to his mom. He asked for my suggestion. What would you tell him?

I needed more answers before giving him a reply. I asked him if his mom's opinion about her brother had changed! After all this, it does make complete sense to hate a person right? Wrong.

Apparently, his mother is still hesitant to even ask what is rightfully theirs. She still believes that he will return everything which he borrowed. She still trusts him. I don't blame her. He doesn't either.

His sister is also too hesitant to question her uncle. What would a rational human being do? My friend had all the right to be angry at his uncle. It has been close to a year since he stopped speaking to his uncle.

I asked him "Not to buy the thali'. Cruel me! I had a good reason. Being denied her thali is the only way she could realize the true face of her own brother. Seeing the missing thali will remind her of the trustworthiness of her brother.

What happens if my friend buys a thali for his own mother whom he loves. His mother will continue to trust her brother as before always as if nothing has changed while her brother could continue to take full financial advantage of her.

My friend's sister is a chartered account and she knows what has been happening as well. She is just too afraid to speak up. My friend is in Spain. What could he possibly do from 8000 km away which his mother and sister cannot possibly do?

My friend still believes that he will get the money back from his uncle. So, I had to dig in deeper. No matter how ugly the truth is. My friend was willing to know it after all "Trust has to be earned".

So, I started asking him questions about his uncle. How much does he earn every month? How is he earning them? What are his assets?

Thinking deeply, my friend replied "He might be earning about 10,000 rupees every month. Definitely not more than that! He is currently running a business which acts as a middleman between the customer and the government to obtain any certificate or document from the government ASAP".

To shed some light upon the truth, I continued "In other words, It would take your uncle approximately 25 years to accumulate the sum of 3,000,000 rupees even if he saved all of the income generated from his business?". I never mentioned about the inflation and the reduction in purchase power of the 3,000,000 rupees, 25 years later but he got the picture.

He replied "Hmm….". Now he was starting to lose hope in ever getting the money back. The idea of his buying a home for his family was starting to fade away. He started to worry about his financial situation for the first time probably in his lifetime. His dreams shattered! He started to get ahold of himself. I could see the pain in his eyes. It deeply saddened me to have done this to him. It was at times like these that I remember "It is sometimes better to let a man live in his dreams, not revealing the truth if you know he is happy there'.

It was too late for me now. I had to end what I had started. So I continued "including the 30 sovereigns of gold which your uncle has borrowed the sum is 3,700,000 rupees which would take your uncle about 30 years to repay and just to return the thali, your uncle needs to save all of his income for 10 months straight".

It would cost around 100,000 rupees to buy a new thali for my friend's mother but his mother was eagerly waiting for his brother to provide her with the means to buy a new thali and my friend was also believing the same till then. I shattered it again!

His uncle was known for his lavish spending. Later, my friend also told me that he is now starting to suspect that his uncle had used a part of the money which his mom gave for safekeeping to renew the house where his uncle currently lives which cost about 1,100,000 rupees. "It was a couple of years ago when my uncle renewed his home. He never muttered a word about the overdraft on the joint fixed deposit then. They deposited it 3 years ago and he clearly had access to those funds" my friend continued.

The total spending accounted for about 1,600,000 rupees. But it still didn't account for the remaining amount. His uncle also mentioned that he has spent a total of 1,800,000 rupees and the remaining Rs.200,000 was loaned to one of his friends and he was expecting it to be returned in a few months.

I asked my friend to ask his uncle to return all the remaining money, whatever he has left of the fixed deposit. He is yet to get a penny from his uncle.

The real cost of not taking control of your financial life! My friend is now starting to take control of his finances. Although the future may seem bleak, he trusts that he could make a difference. He is puffing up his emergency fund now and has a clear road ahead.

1. Save for emergencies
2. Buy a home
3. Sponsor his sister's marriage

That's a good start. It would cost him close to Rs.7,000,000 at the least to make this happen. I am confident that he would be able to do it.

What's your purpose of saving? Without it, don't bother saving. **A purpose backed by strong emotion will push you to succeed in all aspects of your life.**

21

Mark Zuckerberg Didn't Save His Way To Financial Freedom

Why do people think saving is the key to wealth when the most wealthy people didn't get to the top by saving?

A really good question. But it lacks depth. Do you really think that a really talented could achieve peak wealth with the effort which he alone put? The answer is NO.

We all know that even the most talented person could only reach the pinnacle of wealth with the help of their relatives.

Let's take Mark Zuckerberg as an example. He grew up in quite a rich family along with his 3 sisters.

We all do know that Edward Zuckerberg and Karen Kempner Zuckerberg (Parents) tried their best to develop the skills of their talented children. They did hire a tutor, to teach Mark about programming when they noticed that he was interested in programming.

When Mark dropped out of Harvard ($45,958/year for tuition fees alone), his father Edward loaned him money to start the "Facebook".

In short, their parent did all the hard work to push their son to the top, just so that their son can do the remaining effort.

Edward Zuckerberg was a dentist and successfully did his part of the bidding, saved enough money to become wealthy and make sure that their children have an advantage when they start living their life.

You can find this to be true in most of the other successful billionaires.

1. Donald Trump's dad owned thousands of apartment in Queens and New York City (27,000 apartments).
2. Bill Gates's dad (William Henry Gates II) is a retired American attorney and philanthropist and author of the book "Showing Up for Life: Thoughts on the Gifts of a Lifetime".
3. Jeff Bezos who learned his key business skills from his grandfather (who was a very successful scientist, businessman, and landowner)
4. Warren Buffet's father (Howard Homan Buffett) was a successful American businessman, investor, and politician.

Most of the millionaires take hundreds and thousands of dollars from their parents and their grandparents as inheritance / borrow them to get started with their life.

As a matter of fact, you need to own enough shares in your own company when it is going public (IPO).

How will you have enough money if you are just starting out in life?

Exceptions to this rule:

You can always find exceptions to this rule.

1. Steve Jobs, for example, had to even step over / openly take advantage of misfortunes to come to the top which happened to people like Stephen Gary Wozniak. It takes a certain grit to become something from nothing. Steve had it.
2. Jay-Z the famous rapper was a drug dealer and he agrees with it. Luck, skill and ambition to achieve pushed him to make millions.

Others are not so lucky, They have to resort to plain old savings and compounding to take them one step above.

From where your children can pick up and start building more wealth from it. If you happen to fall among the rest, there is only one way to get rich,

1. *Budget* – Spend less than you earn
2. *Save* – Save the rest of the money.
3. *Buy Assets* – Save enough money to buy assets
4. *Optimize returns* – optimize returns on your assets
5. Repeat

> "Every penny saved is a penny earned" – **Benjamin Franklin.**

Honestly, you are doing well if you manage to build on top of your family's wealth. Just make sure that you do not reset yourself back to zero. It is really easy and tempting (I personally know a lot of 'em).

If your parents have done this work for you, better start building more wealth on top of it. Keep building them and provide a higher nest egg to your children with which they can repeat the same.

In my opinion, you are equally successful as Mark Zuckerberg or Warren Buffet if you convert your family's $5000 net-worth to 5 million dollars.

As you know, saving is not the way to create wealth for those who already have enough money to buy assets. Even then the general rule of thumb,

> "Buy Asset – Generate Money From It – Reinvest The Money Generated To Buy More Assets".

In other words, Spend less than you Earn – Save – Buy more assets – Repeat.

DID YOU KNOW THAT A THIRD OF THE LOTTERY WINNERS DECLARE BANKRUPTCY?

According to other sources, it might just be higher. The rule is simple. If you do not know how to manage money, it is useless even if you have a million dollars in your bank account. You will be bankrupt at some point in your life.

Sometimes, it is the people whom you surround yourself with who bring you down.

This is repeated across cultures, border and continents.
There is no use giving the money to the people who are not worth it. It might be a bit rude but it is the truth.

It is hard to become wealthy and harder to remain wealthy.

What are the factors which help people to become and remain wealthy in the first place?

1. You need people around you who push you to the stars and stay with you no matter what.
2. You need to keep learning.
3. You need to become a better personal financial manager.
4. You need to get your life in order / be responsible for your life and take control of your life.

That's just sorting out your personal life. You need to sort out the work aspect of your life as well.

You need to be a better person every day. Continually strive for excellence. Even then there are external factors which could drastically affect your possibility of becoming rich. So you need the plain old **LUCK**.

COMPOUNDING

You need to learn maths and the power of compounding.

This could be the one big game changer for you. As you know, Warren Buffet used it to become wealthy.

As he says, the ideal period for holding a stock is a lifetime. Buy a stock which you know will last for a lifetime with the help of value investing. The table below is for depositing a set amount of money (Rs.12,000) every year for eight years which is also mentioned the *Chapter 19: Home Loan: Is It a Boon In Disguise.*

Year	Total Deposited	Total Interest Earned	Balance
1	Rs.12,000	Rs.593	Rs.12,593
2	Rs.24,000	Rs.2,195	Rs.26,195
3	Rs.36,000	Rs.4,884	Rs.40,884
4	Rs.48,000	Rs.8,749	Rs.56,749
5	Rs.60,000	Rs.13,883	Rs.73,883
6	Rs.72,000	Rs.20,387	Rs.92,387

7	Rs.84,000	Rs.28,372	Rs.112,372
8	Rs.96,000	Rs.37,956	Rs.133,956

The goal is to produce more money with the money which you saved/measure your ROI (Return on Investment).

If you produce > 10% return on investment you are bound to multiply your invested amount 5 times over in a 30-year span.

Remember, **Einstein's Rule of 72**:

Interest Earned x Years Required = 72

It is hard to not speak about the above-mentioned rule while speaking about compounding. For example, you want to double your money in 10 years.

Interest Earned = 72/10 = 7.2%

So, you need to aim for a 7.2% interest rate in order to double your invested money in 10 years. It's as simple as that.

It does not matter if you fail to find a million dollar startup. With the help of compounding, you will definitely quadruple your money invested.

For that, you need to save enough money to invest.

Every financial book speaks about the rule of 72 right? There is an inherent flaw in the equation which nobody speaks about. The equation is fairly accurate for interest rates less than 9% or for the number of years more than 8 years. To understand what I mean, let's have a look at the table below which calculates how long it takes for a $1000 to be doubled for variable interest rates.

Number of Years	Interest Rate	Balance
1	72%	$1,720.00
2	36%	$1,849.60
3	24%	$1,906.62
4	18%	$1,938.78
5	14.4%	$1,959.43
6	12%	$1,973.82
7	10.28%	$1,983.71
8	9%	$1,992.56
9	8%	$1,999.00
10	7.2%	$2,004.23
11	6.454%	$2,009.50
12	6%	$2,012.20

13	5.54%	$2,015.68
14	5.14%	$2,017.21
15	4.8%	$2,020.32

To reduce the error factor, I use a customized version of Einstein's rule of 72 which I had developed. Let's just call it *"Improvised Rule of 72"*.

If you know the number of years, then use this formula:

Number of Years x Interest Rate = 72 + (28 / Number of Years)

The estimated interest rate then is fairly accurate for the first 15 years for a principal amount of $1000 which is evident from the table mentioned below.

Number of Years	Interest Rate	Balance
1	100%	$2,000.00
2	43%	$2,044.90
3	27.1%	$2,053.23
4	19.75%	$2,056.37
5	15.5%	$2,055.46
6	12.7%	$2,049.01

7	10.8%	$2,050.12
8	9.43%	$2,056.32
9	8.34%	$2,056.36
10	7.48%	$2,057.20
11	6.77%	$2,055.61
12	6.19%	$2,055.91
13	5.70%	$2,055.77
14	5.28%	$2,055.14
15	4.92%	$2,055.30

As you can see from the above table, the error margin is now ~ 57 dollars instead of a wide variation of about ~94 to ~ 1 dollars.

This calculation could be used to reliably predict the interest rate required to double your wealth. If you are a person who would like to further reduce the error margin then you should use a much complex version of my formula which reduces the error margin to ~ 7 dollars.

The formula was developed to reliably develop a solution to calculate the interest rate required to double your invested capital when you know the number of years.

This new formula is mentioned below:

Interest Rate Required =
(72 + (28 / Number of Years) / Number of Years) -
(28 / (Number of Years * 10))

The table for the above mentioned formula for a principal amount of $1000 is as follows:

Number of Years	Interest Rate	Balance
1	97.2%	$1,972.00
2	41.6%	$2,005.06
3	26.17%	$2,008.48
4	19.05%	$2,008.71
5	14.96%	$2,007.86
6	12.31%	$2,006.83
7	10.45%	$2,006.48
8	9.08%	$2,004.29
9	8.03%	$2,004.01
10	7.2%	$2,004.23
11	6.52%	$2,003.28
12	5.96%	$2,003.10
13	5.48%	$2,000.84
14	5.08%	$2,001.16

15	4.74%	$2,003.04

Often, the first year produces wrong results. It is expected as the formula promises accurate results for compound interest only and not for simple interest.

Calculating the interest rate for when the number of years > 1 would produce best results as enough time has to be provided to calculate the effect of compounding.

Let me know your comments on the above formula and if you do have a better formula for further reducing the error margin, do let me know. Check my contact details at the end of the book.

22

How to Save Your Way to Achieve Your Dream

There is one thing that we know with certainty, i.e. in today's economic situation a single steady income stream is not enough to sustain a family.

Feudalism supported loyalty; The Lord provided land and safety in exchange for service and loyalty. Communism supported equality; Every person is equal economically and hence ensure everyone is suffering in equal misery or enjoys equal benefits. Capitalism supports competition; You have to be better than the other person while doing the same job in order to excel.

Competition is the only known self-motivator that has been adopted worldwide today. While competition is important so is collaboration among the members of your organization who are working towards the same goal (to get a better share of money from the economy).

In order to achieve this, you and your team have to always compete to provide more in service for the same price. That's the only way the economy moves forward and that means that more is expected of you than was expected the previous year.

The same is expected of your income. You are expected to earn more as the time flies because standing still in today's world is equivalent to going backward.

We are expected to grow with the economy to stay on the same level as we were the previous year.

INVEST IN YOURSELF

Change is the only constant in the economy we live in today. We are often expected to provide more services for the same pay.

It makes complete sense. You have to provide more value to others than what you demand in pay.

> "The only way to make money and stay wealthy is to find a way to do more for others than anyone else is doing which people value" – **Tony Robbins.**

There are people who would like to do the least and expect the most from the society and the economy. This cannot be a reliable strategy as it is not a viable long-term solution to the economic problem.

Providing more in value has its perks. It does not mean that you have to expect less and provide more. For example, if you are currently working in an organization and you want a promotion, the viable strategy to implement would be to do 100% of your work and 50% of your boss' job.

Chances are that in order to do what your boss is doing you have to learn their skill set. Your boss will be much more willing to delegate the work which you are good at than the one you are not.

This forces everyone to always strive to learn. It would be a delight if learning is a pleasurable experience for you.

The days that you wait for the promotion to come to you is gone. You either take what is rightfully yours or stay in the same position and begin to rot.

"We are either growing or dying"

EXPANDING YOUR STREAMS OF INCOME

Another way of generating more income would be to expand your streams of income. Conventional ways of thinking are only going to take you so far.

There are going to be good times and bad times in life. It is better to take advantage of the good times and start building molds around your castle in order to prevent destruction during the bad times.

In the developed nations, you could find organizations which enjoy a monopoly over certain sectors. This is because they have grown too large to be meddled with. There is always a tipping point where a company becomes too large to fail. Similarly, there is a tipping point for every individual's financial situation. At first, it is going to be hard to earn one months income as an extra earning every year.

If we keep at it, keep working on our financial situation, always tweaking to find out what works and what does not for us. We are eventually bound to reach a tipping point after which the money that is produced from your investments or streams of income is more than enough to sustain your current lively hood.

Usually, it takes a million failure and many more attempts to get things right. But more than that we need ideas, capital, willingness to take the risk.

Traveling is one of the most important aspects to gain new ideas. As soon as you get them, write them down somewhere.

Learning a new language, culture, traveling, finding what businesses solve what problems abroad will give you a different perspective of the world. They are often necessary to create better opportunities for ourselves.

The more the problems people solve, the more difficult it is to find a new one. You will be paid in accordance with the value you provide.

After finding a solution to some key problems in life, start providing solutions to those problems and start to innovate, take a major share of the market and start building customer trust. These are the molds that we build around ourselves / businesses.

PAYING LESS TAX

Did you know that you pay less tax when you make money with money than by making money by providing services?

There are ways to pay lesser tax. Always find a way to pay lesser tax if possible.

1. Do not get a home loan because the money and the interest you pay will not be taxed.
2. Do not get a loan in general for the tax benefits.

If you do the calculations, you will know that it is better to pay taxes than to take a loan. If you take a home loan for $100,000 and you pay $12,000 every year for the next 15 years, you will not be paying tax for the $12,000 but you will be paying around $180,000 in the span of 15 years to the banks.

Payment to bank = $12,000 x 15 = $180,000

You pay $80,000 to the bank towards interest alone.

if you pay taxes on the $12,000 for the next 15 years, assuming that the tax will be 30%, you will have.

$8,400 (take home for $12,000) * 15 = $126,000

$180,000 − $126,000 = $54,000

you pay $54,000 to the government in taxes.

There are ways to prevent a certain amount of money from being taxed and help it grow at a steady rate.

Examples are ROTH IRA / IRA in the US, Public Provident Fund (PPF) / Employee Provident Fund (EPF) in India.

I am sure every country has its own name but the point remains the same. You either pay the government or invest in the stock market before you obtain your pay. Hence that sum will not be accounted for taxes.

Beware though as some of the schemes tax the money when you withdraw from that account.

Employee Provident Fund and Public Provident Fund in India do not tax upon withdrawal.

ROTH IRA in the US demands the tax to be paid while entering the fund but has a tax-free growth once the money is in the ROTH IRA.

IRA in the US demands a tax to be paid upon withdrawal.

> "It is always better to pay the taxes before growth than after growth"

You will be paying more otherwise.

SAVING MORE BY CUTTING SPENDING

One of the first things to do while starting to save is to cut spending. it is so easy to say but so hard to implement.

It is often considered as a no-brainer. You will have to forego on a lot of things. Cut all of your unnecessary expenses. Live with the bare minimum. Start saving money.

While you are at it, the first few months will be the hardest as you will see very less result for your hard work.

You keep at it for a few months / a few years. You will start to see the results.

DOUBLING DOWN ON WHAT WORKS FOR YOU

There are things which will yield maximum results for your neighbor but will yield none for you. Learn to accept the fact that you are better at certain things in life and others are better at certain other things.

You can try a lot of things at a given time or give your best on one thing. It is better to start working on the things that you do best without deviating.

If something works for you, better double down on it till you get the maximum juice out of it. Keep at it till you can get no more from it. Then you will start to get a steady stream of income from that work.

Always work on generating passive income from your business. It is one of the most basic principles for generating multiple streams of income.

One of the important passive income streams is through investing in a business. The investment can be in the form of stock market purchase, mutual fund purchase, index fund or building your own business.

It takes time to build your own business from scratch. It is all the easier to buy an already established business if you are short on time in order to generate income.

Another better example of doubling down on what you are good at is trying to get a better return on your investment for the same amount of risk for the same amount of money.

> "Can anybody imagine a time where times were not hard and money not scarce" – **Ralph Walford Emerson.**

Generating money is a hard task. That's exactly why many settle down for good enough returns.

Best yields can be generated for the opportunistic. To obtain the best results you need to analyze what you currently have and learn to appreciate the things which you currently have and are good at.

Improve on what you are good at and delegate the tasks you are bad at. You only have a finite amount of time with you. You cannot possibly imagine doing all the things on your own.

That's exactly why businesses are for. You can pay them to do your work for you.

PLANNING TO ACHIEVE YOUR DREAM

> "When you cease to dream, you cease to live "- **Malcolm Forbes.**

What happens after you start generating some money from the above-said strategies?

You start to give the money a name, a purpose. Everything in life needs a purpose. What happens to the money you do not give a name to? You would eventually waste it away.

We dream of buying things and consuming them in our lives. What if we find a way to save money for spending it eventually on the dreams.

Tony Robbins calls it DREAM BUCKET. What are the things that you could only dream of having right now but want it really bad enough?

1. List the most important dreams in your life.
2. Allocate the newly generated resources to aid in the attainment of the dream.
3. Keep at it till you achieve enough capital.

The greatest advantages of dreaming to attain something is that it requires a great deal of effort, innovation, problem solving and luck. If you really want it bad enough you will plan for it and execute a detailed plan to attain it.

As long as it could be obtained in a way which would be beneficial for all parties concerned, it should be possible.

GRASS IS GREENER ON THE OTHER SIDE

Appreciating what you currently hold dear is just as important as dreaming and chasing your dream.

It could be a foolish move if you choose to chase your dream without realizing what you would like to never miss in your life. I could remember a huge number of people who have made that mistake and are regretting it now.

A classic example is a relative of mine. Let's call him Kevin. Kevin was a physiotherapist. He was working in Chennai, India for a few years after which he got a really good offer in Kuwait. It was the best financial move for him and life was happy for a few years until Kevin's parents started seeking an alliance.

We still practice arranged marriages in India where parents would seek alliance and ask their children to marry them. It was back in 2003 when the "US invasion of Iraq" began. Bombshells would hit the country of Kuwait. So people were afraid to marry him as it would mean that the girl goes to Kuwait and risks her life.

Having searched for an alliance for years unsuccessfully, the family members of Kevin arranged for a new job in Dubai. A much safer country when compared to Kuwait back in the days of Iraq war. Kevin finally got married and was successfully working in Dubai. Even though the salary wasn't much, his wife would also aid him financially by working in Dubai. It was a happy family. They couldn't save a lot but they were getting along.

I honestly do not know what hit them. After eight years in Dubai as a physiotherapist, Kevin moved back to India. I could only imagine that such a move had a more emotional explanation than a rational explanation. That was when I was doing my undergraduate and even I knew at that time that it was a wrong decision! I even told them but what's the use of telling them after they have moved to India.

Now, he had borrowed 1,000,000 rupees to rent a space and make it a hospital to treat patients. Don't ask me what happened to the savings which Kevin had while he was working in Dubai.

I should only imagine that they had spent it all and came back to India empty-handed. Probably lived an extravagant life or earned too little. I would never know and Kevin was not exactly transparent about his financial situation with anyone.

So, Kevin's new hospital is being totally new and only starting to attract new customers. It had been one year since Kevin opened a new hospital in India. As you know, any hospital requires reputation and Kevin was by all means building his own reputation in

India. He was also very stubborn about building his from scratch. One could only wonder why!

He also had an opportunity to buy a 10-year-old hospital with regular customers at a much affordable price which he instantly denied.

It all turns out to be a mistake only when you give up. It is never a wrong decision until you give up! Kevin gave up on Dubai. It was the wrong decision. Kevin gave up on building his reputation in India and migrated to Canada a couple of years later.

That was about the time when I traveled to the UK for my Masters. Kevin was in his 40's and he had an 8-year-old kid at that time. He imagined a better place in Canada. Till today, He is working as a part-time physiotherapist and could not find a more permanent job, During his stay in Canada, Kevin had another child. They are now a happy family of four.

For their migration, they had borrowed another 500,000 rupees more. Now, they owe a grand total of 1,500,000 rupees. How could Kevin repay the amount in full when he is struggling financially?

Borrowing from relatives has its own perks. You do not have to pay interest on the money borrowed but when you fail to repay the money promptly, you risk losing the relationship. I guess that's what happened with Kevin. He lost the people close to him because he wanted a financial shelter under their roof.

He is now slowly starting to repay the borrowed amounts but the damage has already been done.

Everyone looks to him as a person who had missed the opportunity to be someone better.

Kevin acknowledges the fact as well. He often regrets leaving Dubai and says "My junior is now managing the whole physiotherapist department. If only I had been there!".

It is sometimes wise to plant your roots and settle down in a single place if you know you are doing reasonably good there.

It makes sense then to say "The grass is not always greener on the other side; It may seem to, but in reality, it is not".

23

Buying a Car the Right Way

Every plan, savings or budget is personalized and cannot be implemented by your neighbor. It won't be the right fit for them. So is your car.

1. Which car should you buy? A Ferrari? A Toyota? or a Mini Cooper?
2. Do you want it new or don't mind if it is a few years old?
3. Is a 2 seater enough for you? How about a 5 seater?
4. Do you want to buy a petrol or a diesel engine?
5. Do you usually travel long distances? Is it for driving within the city limits?

You can personalize it even further by wanting a sunroof/convertible.

The concept of buying a car the right way depends on one's financial situation. Ask yourself before buying a car.

1. Do I already have an emergency fund in place?

2. Are you going to pay all cash for the car?

Both the answers to the above questions should be a yes before choosing to buy a car.

WHY SHOULDN'T YOU PAY FOR THE CAR WITH A LOAN?

The minute you take the car out of the showroom the price of the car goes down by a minimum of 30% to 50%.

If you have a loan you should be paying an interest on the loan. How much is it that you are paying? And how long are you going to pay?

For the convenience of traveling in your car is it worth paying $200 / $300 every month excluding fuel and parking charges?

Would you rather be a little less comfortable traveling on a public transport and saving $150 to $250 till you have saved enough to buy a car?

Chances are that if you start the practice of saving the money to buy a car you will end up buying a second-hand car.

And you will feel just as happy as buying a new car.

Choose to be financially free especially when it comes to paying for depreciating assets.

The general rule of thumb is to save one year's worth of income for buying a car.

Is that not enough? Maybe you could choose a cheaper model and settle for a second hand or better yet, increase your income!

COMFORT AND PRESTIGE

We choose to buy a car because we want to be comfortable, not getting constrained by the time limits of public transport and generally wanting to save time.

We will end up saving about one to a maximum of two hours everyday by traveling in a car.

What Will You Use These Hours For?

Would you rather spend the time watching TV, Browsing / Cooking your tomorrow's lunch?

An average man watches TV / uses a mobile phone for over 4 hours a day.

But browsing is pleasurable for us and for most of them waiting in traffic in a car is not.

Would you trade $250 every month for getting enough time to browse / cook / whatever you want to do?

That's exactly what you are doing when you buy a car which you can't afford instead of traveling in a public transport for a few years.

But I am getting a car am I not?

Yes. But is the car worth the money which you are paying for? It is depreciating everyday, every time you use and every extra mile it moves.

You are better off with a second-hand car with less mileage. It would do the same job and you would end up not spending 50% more for the same car just because it was not used before.

People also buy a car for the prestige of owning it.

We all would like to be treated well and the people who judge you often judge you by the appearances and it includes the car you drive.

What is the car that fits your standard and appeases your pride?

If you are from a middle class or having a rich background owning a car is a basic requirement and is often taken for granted.

Do you earn as much and save as much?

The truth is if your financial situation is bad, as in case, you go into debt for buying a depreciating asset and cannot repay it within the next 5 years, you don't deserve to buy a car as long as it is not absolutely impossible to commute without it.

24

Never Kill Your Golden Goose

What does secured capital mean? It means **Minimum Risk and Maximum Security** to me.

These are the most common ways to kill your Golden Goose.

1. Bad investment thereby losing the capital and potential return.
2. Secured capital and promised return but you spend your interest earned.
3. Born poor, lived modestly, spent everything and died poor. (Never tried to make a golden goose)

There is another way to kill your golden goose before making one, without even knowing you are killing it "by being trapped in a cycle of creating and destroying your savings". It renders the process of building your golden goose useless.

BURDEN OF DEBT

I have seen a lot of people who are never too serious about their goals in life. If you are not serious about your intentions and what you would like to do with your money, no other being will give a serious thought about it.

Everybody dreams of buying a new home but how many ever see it to the completion without ever having to get a bank loan?

Why is housing loan bad anyway? Ask yourself: What is the probability of your not going through a crisis in the period that you are repaying the loan? (10 years, 15 years or 25 years)

For me, the possibility of experiencing a financial crisis in a 25 year period is 100%.

> "Never pay for your Current Desires with your Future Income"

It is going to be really hard to shake the home loan off once you take it.

Everyone is attached to his or her home. We see it as our home. It's a pride of possession to be possessive about. But is it really yours when somebody can take it away from you if you do not pay them for a certain amount of time?

I am here promoting that the debt is unnecessary for anybody but what the heck will the economy do without a debt?

The whole system relies on DEBT. If there is no DEBT, there is no money in the system to circulate.

Have you watched the video about how the economic money machine works?

A link is provided in *Chapter 16 : Debt Analysis: Analysing Your Financial Past.* Do watch it!

> "You don't need to be in Debt if the money in debt is not generating more than what you have to pay for it."

BALL AND CHAIN

Have you ever felt that however hard that you try to save in order to build your golden goose it becomes much more futile?

If you have not, then you are the lucky few whose life is nurtured the right way.

Chances are that some circumstances or people in your life are sucking the golden goose dry as soon as you make them. Whom to blame? You are to blame. Yes!

> "If you are born poor it's not your mistake; but if you die poor it's your mistake" – **Bill Gates.**

The choices that we make in our life have a pattern. We all have our preferences in life. The pattern in life can be consciously made or it may be a habit which we obtain from our parents, loved ones or whomever we spent the most time with.

Bad habits, i.e. the habits that are detrimental to our financial and personal life seep into our lives if we are not too bothered about whom we spend the most time with.

It will be hard to shake off the habit once it becomes a part of your identity. People start expecting it from you and you find some pleasure in doing it.

Maybe it's your loved ones who are draining your Golden goose dry.

Analyse who has the power to sap the golden goose dry. Make sure they are synergising with you and that you both are on the same page.

It's of no use if one is trying to build a home while the other person is trying to use the same pool of resource for something else.

DESTRUCTION IN DISGUISE

Have you ever meant to help someone in money trouble by lending them some amount of money and ended up losing the relationship and the money?

Even the right intention can be a wrong decision if money is involved.

The questions to ask yourself when someone is borrowing money from you are:

1. Does he have a current income source from which he could easily repay the amount in the time frame that he has promised to repay?
2. Does the person have the intention to repay?

3. Where does the money go? Is he borrowing it to consume or produce?
4. What is the immediate crisis which makes the money necessary?

How could you be polite while saying "no" to the lending? Saying "NO" to lending at dire moments in life can be disastrous to the relationship if done at the wrong time and in the wrong situation.

Friends and families are there to help each other in times of hardship and struggle both emotionally and financially if necessary. But lending too much money at the wrong time to the right person for them to consume an unnecessary merchandise which will add no value to the borrower will have repercussions if the borrower does not have the intention/income to repay the borrowed sum of money.

Another question to ask is: Which is the source of money?

1. Is it from your emergency fund?
2. Is it from your golden goose?

It is not too much money if the money lent can be generated by you in a few months.

If you are lending from your emergency fund, you are essentially losing your security of emergency fund temporarily to support your friend/family in need.

Of course, you earn the trust and reliability from your friend/family. But are they the kind of persons who keep up their end of the bargain?

MISERY LOVES COMPANY

Have you ever noticed that some people are always in the state of emergency, always facing mishaps in life? They are always a few hundred dollars short every month.

I personally know a handful of persons who are always short on money; but why?

They care the least about money. I have asked them why are you least bothered about money? You know what they say?

"Money comes; money parts. But relationships are for fostering and nurturing."

Well, I say "misery loves company". These people will stay broke and long to stay broke together.

They are getting exactly what they bargained in life. They are trading money for the comfort of staying broke with their friends/relatives.

CAN SOMEONE BE COMFORTABLY BROKE?

One feels at home when people who have the same mindset get together. You never want to leave them ever. They become your best friends and next of kin.

That's a comfort circle someone is building for themselves. Inside that zone, everyone stays the same and on par. If someone steps up, he is either pulled down or has the necessity to pull the circle to the new level which he has reached or leave the comfort zone which he was a part of and start a new life.

> "The fear of losing loved ones in the future is much painful than losing money today."

PAYING FOR YOUR COMFORT ZONE

It requires a good amount of vision and perseverance to achieve something in life. Life is going to be hard. You are going to lose the things you thought will be there with you for a lifetime.

Life is unpredictable. You can control it in two ways:

1. By letting fear control you and paying a premium fee to stay in your comfort zone and keeping others close together without letting them fly away.
2. Exploring the life in ways you would like to, by having a clear vision of where you are going and where you would like to.

You will be living a terribly unhappy life if you do not shape the life as you want it to be and by letting fear control you because "Change is the only constant in life".

"Fear shouldn't paralyse us but has to motivate us" - **Salvation, TV Series.**

BONUS

Financial Goals to Achieve Before You Turn 35

You must have come across a recent study which suggests that you must have saved twice your annual salary before you reach the age of 35 in order to ensure that you retire by 67 having to live a similar lifestyle afterward. As many agree and as many disagree, The fact still remains the same.

We start earning when we are about 25 and by the time we have reached 10 years of our working life, it is only reasonable to expect that one has saved about 2 years of one's annual salary.

A minimum of one in three persons could expect to live till their 80's which requires a minimum of 15 years after his retirement to be sponsored by the 30 + years of his working life.

Having said that, it is only fair to expect that you have at least 2 years of your annual income as savings/investment by the time you reach 35 (assuming you have a private pension).

How do we achieve that figure?

Let's take for example: That you take 10% of your income and invest in Apple Stocks from the start of 2008 until now (2018).

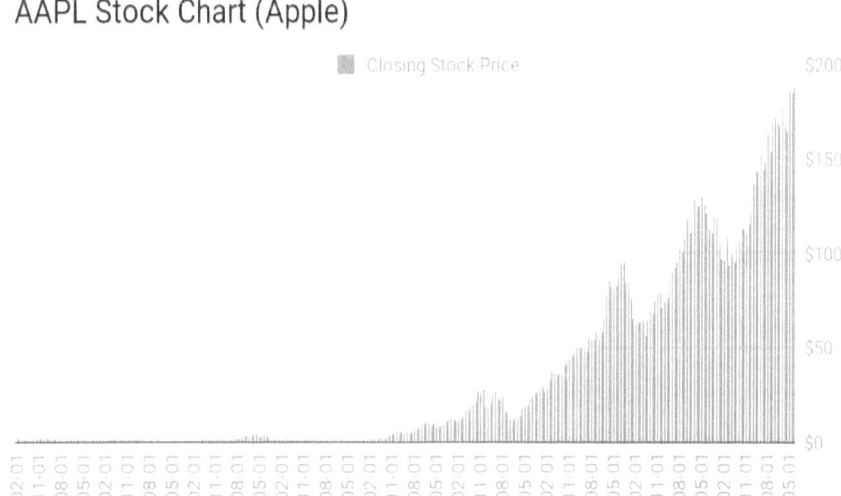

AAPL Stock Chart (Apple)

The table below explains how you could have saved up to 3.6 times your annual income assuming that your salary is $35,000 and that you save $300 every month.

Stock	AAPL
Type of Investment	Dollar Cost Averaging
Start Date	07/11/2008
End Date	03/27/2018

Dollar Cost Averaging Interval	1 month
Amount to Invest Every Month	$300
Initial Investment	$300
Total Invested Capital	$35,100.00
Annual Return (%)	25.29%
Final Net Worth	$128,032.03

Although the above mentioned table is a hypothetical example, it provides a reasonable estimate of the power of savings and investments with Dollar Cost Averaging.

BEING PAID FOR YOUR VALUE

Negotiating your salary is a conversational skill which can be improved.

The sooner you get paid more the better it is.

Earning more soon will directly impact your possibility of a happy retirement. The initial 10 years of your growth and savings contribute up to 4 -12 years of your retirement if invested on a proper vessel.

However, the later investments have the potential to compensate 2-6 years of your retirement assuming all the savings are 10% and are invested in a growing stock/index fund.

Not having your salary rise now could cost you up to 4 – 12 years of your retirement savings, That's an unbelievably high amount for a small 5 – 10% rise. All thanks to the power of compounding.

No one is born with an inbuilt talent to negotiate. It is a skill which is developed as you keep practicing.

The more you practice your skills on negotiation, the better the chances you have at not chasing your payment on bills down the line.

Inform your intention of getting a raise to your boss. Chances are that he has to discuss them with other colleagues in your company. Inform your boss well in advance, tell them how you have brought value to the company while being a team player and how excited are you about the work you do in the same organization.

While getting a raise do not just think about raising your base salary, think about the possibility of including stock compensation, vacation days, insurance, tax-free benefits and other possibilities while negotiating.

HAVE A FULL FLEDGED, PRACTISING PERSONAL FINANCIAL PLAN

It is mandatory to have a full roadmap of your personal financial life before you turn 35.

The financial plan would include your short-term goals, mid-term goals and long-term goals. It serves as a way of measuring your goals vis a vis where you are right now.

Without a proper measuring tool (your Personal Financial Roadmap), you will be lost.

Do you know anybody who was lost in a forest? Ask them what happened. It is most likely that it was next to impossible to get out of it without having a proper plan which includes measuring something (Sun/Stars).

They generally walk in circles only to find out that they have walked back to where they have started.

This exact scenario is true in personal financial life as well. If you do not have a proper roadmap and vision, you would end up walking in circles.

HAVING SAVED 6 – 12 MONTHS WORTH OF INCOME AS EMERGENCY FUND

We are sure that you would have ended up in a financially daunting situation in 10 + years of your work life like a shortage of money, your getting fired or staying jobless for a month or two.

It is only rational to believe that you should be saving a minimum of 6 months of your monthly salary as an emergency fund.

If not, it is guaranteed that you would end up struggling a lot when things go south.

Emergency fund acts as a security between you and any financial situation. This is reflected in how you see life itself and can directly impact how you work.

DEDICATING A PORTION OF YOUR INCOME

TOWARDS YOUR RETIREMENT

By 35, you should have already started saving a portion of your salary consistently towards your retirement.

Your initial investment between 25 years of age and 35 years of age will go a long way in determining how soon you will be able to retire.

Below is an example of how age plays a role in how soon you retire if you save $3,600 every year in monthly installments in an investment with an initial deposit of $3600 in year 0.

Year	Total Deposits	Total Interest	Balance

1	$7,100	$434	$7,534
5	$21,500	$5,666	$27,166
10	$39,500	$22,441	$61,941
15	$57,500	$55,536	$113,036
20	$75,500	$112,611	$188,111
25	$93,500	$204,921	$298,421
30	$111,500	$349,003	$460,503
35	$129,500	$569,154	$698,654
40	$147,500	$901,076	$1,048,576

From the above mentioned table, we can find out that the money has more than doubled in the successive 10 years (30 – 40 years) from $460,503.27 to $1,048,576.99.

So, this could be the key to maintaining your current lifestyle throughout your retired life in lieu of living the last few years penniless.

The ideal age to start saving for your retirement is 25, although you ought to keep in mind that it is never too late.

HAVING MULTIPLE SOURCES OF SECURE INCOME

Finally, having multiple sources of income is a sure shot way to make your life stress free and secure.

1. Have a passive stream of income. *(check out Pat Flynn's website for more information about building a passive online business)*
2. Build a nest egg which generates money for you.
3. Rent out your second home.
4. Invest in Index Funds.
5. Develop new skills

All these are some of the ways to generate multiple streams of income. Sure, they come with their own risks. Tell me what doesn't?

Part Six

Investment Management Strategy

26

Investment Management Strategy

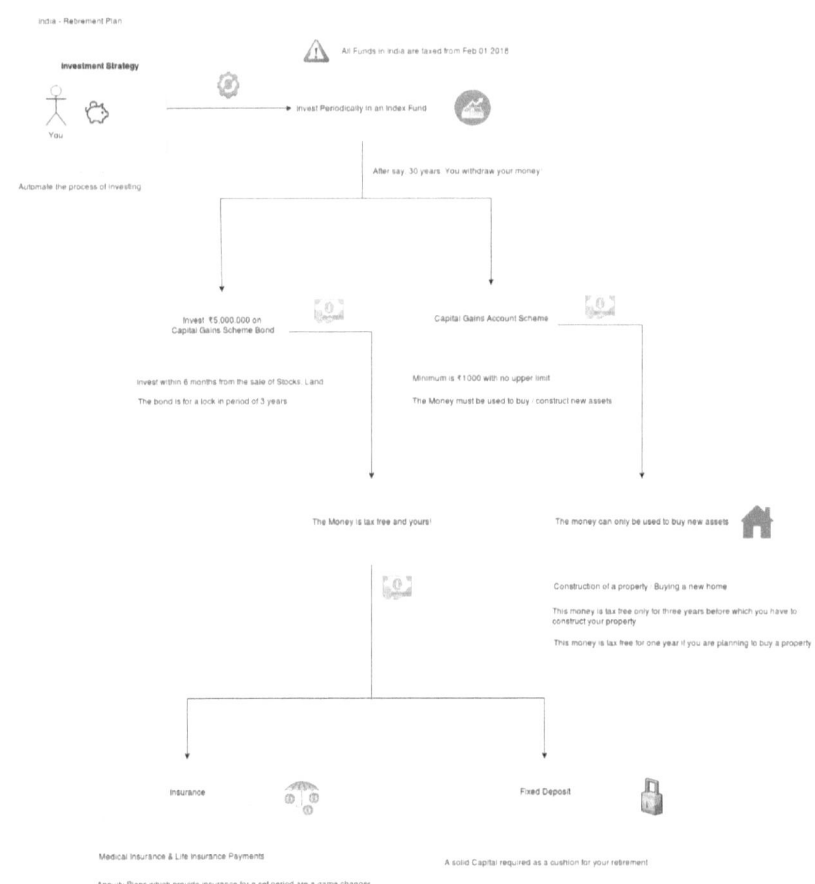
Investment Strategy Example Blueprint
readerb.com

The investment management strategy has to be personalized and should satisfy your need. For this reason, I do not provide a tailor-made strategy which could satisfy everyone's needs.

Find the link to the above mentioned investment strategy blueprint below:

https://readorb.com/wp-content/uploads/2018/08/Investment-Strategy-India.png

The above mentioned strategy is a sample blueprint which could be implemented by any individual in India.

I believe that the above example would shed some light on how to invest. Let's take a retirement plan in India. Apart from your mandatory payments to the Employees Provident Fund (EPF), let's imagine that you are having a surplus and are choosing to invest in an index fund (UTI Nifty Fund) a set amount periodically and systematically. In other words, you are investing in UTI Nifty Fund with Rupee Cost Averaging strategy.

After you retire, you are withdrawing all of the balance from the UTI Nifty Fund and are choosing to do it in a cost efficient manner.

You could split the investment into two if not three separate sections.

1. First 5,000,000 rupees from the UTI Fund Investment goes into a Capital Gains Scheme Bond which is offered through National Highway Authority of India (NHAI) & Rural Electric Corp. (REC).
2. Second split which could be any amount which you desire is necessary to build a home goes into a Capital Gains Account Scheme.
3. Third split is left in the UTI Nifty Fund untouched to grow.

Wait for the first 5,000,000 rupees which is invested in the Capital Gains Scheme Bond to mature. It has a maturity period of 3 years, after which you could invest the capital gained which is legal and tax-free into Fixed Deposit & Annuity Plans.

If you are building a home, you have a three year period before which you have to use the money invested in the Capital Gains Account Scheme. You have to use it only for that purpose and the government will make sure of it. So, build the house for you to live or better build one with the sole intention of renting it.

The third section which we have left it in the UTI Nifty Fund could be taken after the first investment in the Capital Gains Scheme Bond have matured, because the total aggregate maximum investment allowed in these bonds are capped at 5,000,000 rupees. You can keep repeating this cycle to retrieve the investment from the index funds free of tax in India.

Else, you will be liable for taxes on the capital gains. We should make sure that wherever possible we legally avoid all the taxes.

Indian government have provided us with EPF and PPF which could be considered as a boon. Other countries do not have such schemes and we can consider ourselves lucky as the growth within the EPF & PPF are not taxed along with the invested capital.

Roth IRA & IRA are taxed one way or the other while ROTH IRA requires tax paid dollars to be invested, traditional IRA requires the employee to pay tax upon withdrawal.

Further explanation is provided in the *Chapter 28 : Investing in Index Funds.*

27

Investing in Mutual Funds

Mutual funds also known as actively managed funds are the most sorted out forms of investments by the public.

The general interest towards the mutual fund being "You do not know the rules of investing in a mutual fund; let the professionals take care of your money and we will beat the market."

Mutual funds are managed by a professional investor for the profit of the organization he is working under and not for the clients who invest the money with them.

While choosing a mutual fund, we usually choose the best performing funds. Out of all, Morningstar provides a reasonable estimate of the best performing fund for the current year by segregating them in stars, 5-star funds being the best performing and 1-star funds being the worst performing.

This estimate cannot be reliably predicted for long-term performance of a mutual fund because the mutual funds fail in the long term and do not beat the market returns in the short term. Check out

"Common sense on mutual fund investing" by John C Bogle for more information.

According to Bogle, the expense ratio is not a reliable estimate to predict the cost of a mutual fund as there are hidden costs involved. The total costs involved in mutual fund investing are

1. Marketing Costs
2. Tax costs
3. Planned administration cost
4. Cash Drag
5. Redemption Fees
6. Exchange Fees
7. Account fee
8. Purchase fee

Generally, the cost of the fund is more than 2% and as high as 4% of the potential returns.

They generally charge you even if the investment fails to perform.

The best argument against the mutual fund is from Tony Robbins book, "Money - Master the Game".

1. 48% of the actively managed fund managers in the US do not invest their money themselves. They would do so if they believe that their funds perform well.
2. The investors deem a fund to be a suitable investment. Do you ever settle for something that is suitable in life? like a suitable house, suitable meal?

The mutual funds are often suggested by financial advisers. They often do receive a percentage of your investment capital as commission. Never go through a financial adviser. As going through them will often include brokerage fees. They are included in the mutual fund costs.

WHY ARE PEOPLE INTERESTED IN MUTUAL FUNDS?

In the US, Mutual funds are tied to retirement savings (401K). They are often the most sorted investments in India as well by some sectors of the society often due to lack of knowledge on the hidden cost and the underperformance of the funds.

People often go with the majority and start to buy stocks when the emotions and hopes are high in the market. That is when the mutual funds cost more to buy.

They often sell the mutual fund holdings within the year due to low performance. The chase for performance in this era is never ending and the only person who is bound to lose is the person who is investing.

It's not called investing when you buy high and sell low. It's expecting and speculating.

Do you ever buy a commodity for $2 and plan to sell it for $1 with the intention of making a profit?

Isn't that what majority of the people do when they buy and sell the stocks?

WHAT ABOUT OTHERS WHO SAVE FOR THE RETIREMENT WITH THE MUTUAL FUNDS?

The first question involved is how much are you paying in costs to the mutual funds?

Did you know that there are options to pay the tax on the mutual funds before and let the money raise tax-free in the US and in India?

The retirement account will have a stunted growth due to the payment of costs. Costs cannot be taken lightly as 2- 4% of the cost can account for more than 70% of your potential earning for the retirement account.

The performance of the market is illustrated in the below mentioned graph. The total percentage of growth every year for S&P 500 Total Return is 11.37 percentage from 1988 to 2017.

If you had bought one share of S&P 500 Total Return in 1988 for 276.856 dollars, the invested capital would have become 4689.608 dollars, a growth rate of 1593.87% for a 30 year period from 1988 to 2017 assuming that you reinvest all the dividends earned.

S&P 500 Total Returns

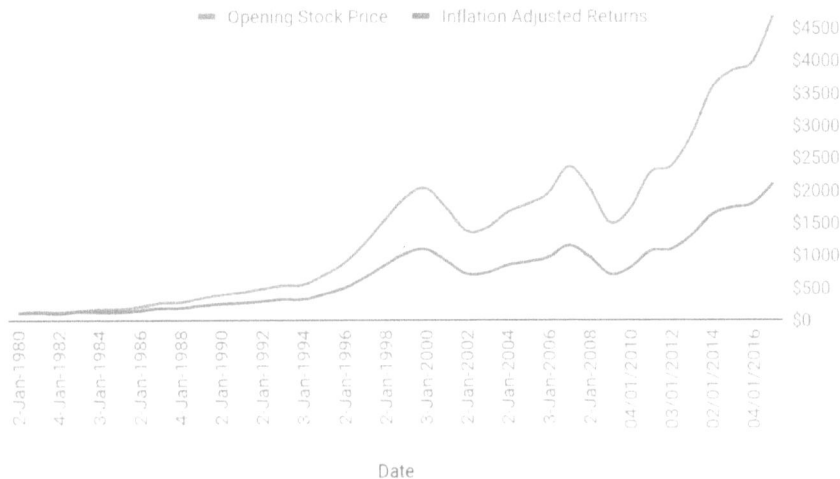

The graph below mentions the inflation in the United States and India between 1988 to 2017 calculated by Consumer Price index formula. The United States inflation is much more contained at 78% for the period of 30 years when compared to other developing nations. In other words, the value of 1 dollar in 1988 is $1.78 in 2017.

The gain of 1593.87% for S&P 500 Total Returns mentioned above is the nominal growth. The gain is not inflation adjusted. After adjusting for inflation the percentage of growth for S&P 500 total return is 850.976% with dividends reinvested. The gain is mainly due to the growth of every business in the S&P 500.

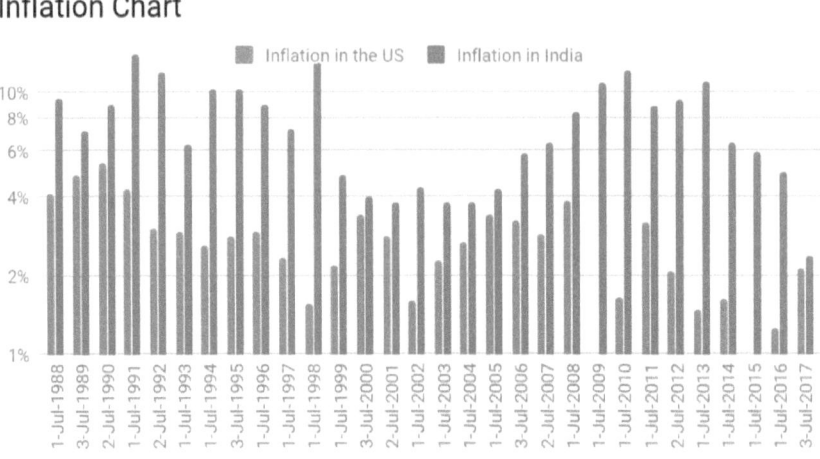

We should keep in mind that S&P 500 is an index and mutual funds that follow the index are called Index Funds. They are a whole different category of funds which we will discuss in the next section.

MUTUAL FUND NOMINAL RETURNS VS REAL RETURNS

The below graph shows the returns generated by FFIDX Mutual funds for a period between 1980 – 2017. The FFIDX mutual fund returns growth is 174% for the past 38 years which is about 17% inflation-adjusted gain. The performance of the fund is average according to morning star with a 3-star rating. The fund invests 95 percent in stocks out of which some are high-risk category stocks. It is an incredibly risky stock which started in the 1930's.

If the mutual fund has an average or a bad performance you might lose money in the long term instead of earning. Also, keep in mind the taxes incurred on the earnings.

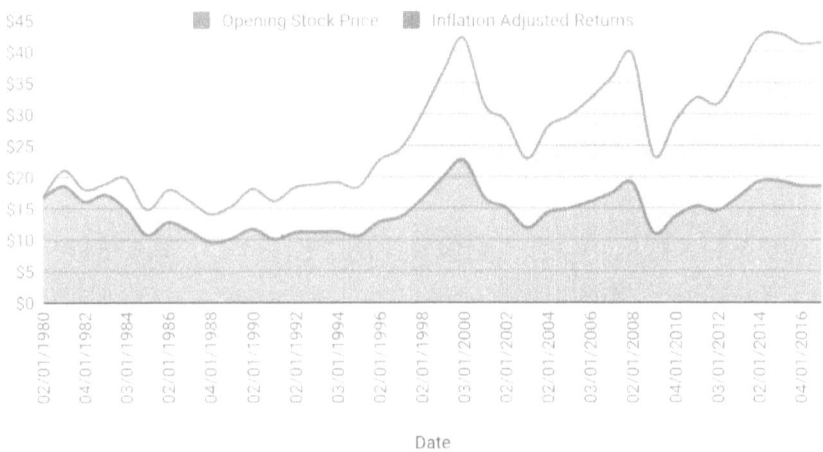

If you find your mutual fund to be average, you should leave the money already invested in the fund and start a separate investment to an index fund. The tax payment on the stunted growth is not worth paying. It is worthwhile to let it grow and let compounding take care of the rest.

The poor performance of the mutual fund can either be due to the higher cost or poor asset allocation strategies by the fund managers. There are tax burdens involved in trading the stocks by the fund managers as well. These are hidden costs involved with mutual funds. They are directly charged from the investors.

The expense ratio of the FFIDX is only 0.52% but the growth rate cannot simply be explained by the expense ratio alone. Such a low expense ratio must yield great returns on the investment. It fails due to the active management and speculation.

By comparison, this is the worst form of investment for retirement account as it barely keeps up with inflation compared to the S&P 500 Total Returns index.

WHY DO WE CALCULATE INFLATION-ADJUSTED RETURNS INSTEAD OF NOMINAL RETURNS?

When we invest our money, we invest it in hope that the current purchase power of the money will grow.

As time goes by, the same amount of money is going to buy you less of something. It is necessary to adjust the returns to account for inflation in order to calculate the real increase in the purchasing power of the money that you invested.

By calculating the real increase in the purchasing power of your invested capital after tax, we will know how much you exactly earned through that investment. That is the true measure of potential returns on an investment.

COMPARISON OF AFTER-TAX RETURNS

The long-term capital gains in India from equity shares, units of the business trust and mutual funds are not taxed as long as you have not invested in Debt Mutual Funds.

The long-term capital gains in the US are not taxed for those who fall under the 10% and 15% income tax bracket but the wealthiest can be charged as high as 20% in taxes. If the capital gain is more than $200,000 an additional tax of 3.8% applies on top of the capital gains tax rates.

Dividends are taxed in the US based on your income tax rates.

Taxes cannot be generalized, The above information is collected on 2018 and is subjected to change but knowing how you will be taxed on the capital gains is mandatory.

If you are planning to sell your shares do not forget to calculate the capital gain tax.

SHOULD YOU INVEST IN A MUTUAL FUND?

Do you find any mutual fund which could keep up with the growth of S&P 500?

Finding one with a 30-year-old history is hard enough, given the number of funds that fail to perform at all.

Did you choose a fund that keeps up close enough to the returns provided by S&P 500?

How is its track record? How did it perform in the long run? How long since its inception?

Rarely do the funds keep up with the S&P 500 and even when they do, it is even rarer to find one which keeps performing on a consistent basis.

There are better options available to invest rather than a mutual fund for retirement savings or any long-term investments for that matter.

28

Investing in Index Funds

Index funds are low-cost funds which do not require any active management.

They typically follow an index and their primary agenda is to reduce the tracking error of the fund.

A really good index fund has a minimum tracking error.

Since they do not need any fund managers the cost of managing the funds are really low as well.

The expense ratios of the funds are typically below one percentage point.

The asset management of the index fund would involve maintaining the same ratio of stocks as the index it follows.

Index funds are as close as anyone can get to secure 100% of the market returns.

Just like mutual funds, the index funds can only be sold or bought based on the previous days closing stock prices.

This is designed in such a way as these types of funds are unfit for day to day trading purposes.

The ideal scenario for holding a share of an index fund would be holding it for the long term according to John C Bogle. He was the first to start an index fund. His organization Vanguard is the leading provider of index funds today.

It is also one of the largest mutual fund companies with over 4.5 trillion dollars in assets under management.

The cost impact of the index fund with 10% average returns spanning over 3 decades and assuming that its cost is 1% would be 10% of the market returns in one year, 14% of the market returns in a decade and 24% of the market returns in 25 years.

We should also keep in mind that the goal of investing is to capture 100% of the market returns.

THE BEST INDEX FUND

Selecting an index fund is equivalent to selecting a simplistic straightforward fund with minimum charges.

All index funds were not created equal. Some are to be avoided at all costs.

Index funds that carry a sales load or commission, for example. It does not make sense to pay a front-end load or a back-end load in an index fund. The sales load is a straightforward cost which is to be avoided given the fact that the index funds with no load are available.

Front-end sales load is a fee to enter the fund, usually a percentage of invested capital. For example, if you are investing $5000 in an index fund with a sales load of 5%, you would have to pay $5250 to enter the fund and the $250 would be the front-end sales load.

Similarly, the back-end sales load is a fee that is charged to exit the fund usually a percentage of invested capital. For example, an investment of $5000 has grown to $10,000 and upon withdrawal, the index fund is charging you a back-end sales load of 5%. You would have to pay $500 upon withdrawal of $10,000.

Front-end sales load is the least evil of both loads as you will be paying a straight fee before your money has grown.

The backend sales load is the worst of all evil as you would be paying a percentage of the total money being withdrawn. Usually, the invested money would have grown many folds in an index fund. You would be paying a lot of money compared to the front end load.

The best fund would be a no-load fund with minimal hidden fees like marketing fees, brokerage fees and an expense ratio less than 0.50%.

All returns calculated by the fund managing companies are pre-tax returns. Although the industries ignore taxes, they take a major chunk of the market returns. As high as 20% in some of the cases. So it makes sense to hold an index fund in a non-taxable account.

In the US, the best option would be to buy an index fund with the above-mentioned criteria through an IRA or better yet through ROTH IRA.

TAX EXEMPTIONS IN INDIA

In India, the long-term capital gains tax would be 20%. Irrespective of your age you will be taxed. Above the flat 20% tax, you may be subjected to additional 3% of tax for educational cess. It is a tax levied upon the investor to help sponsor government programs and is collected independently of other taxes.

On top of that, there maybe a surcharge of up to 15% depending on the income slab of the individual.

So you would be paying about 23% to 38% of the long-term capital gains on taxes alone. To avoid paying such a high amount of taxes you could avail tax exemptions.

Age Exemption

Depending on your age, you could be exempted from long-term capital gains of up to 500,000 rupees.

1. For resident individual aged 80 or above, one could avail 500,000 rupees exemption for Long-Term Capital Gains.
2. For resident individual aged 60 or above, one could avail 300,000 rupees exemption for Long-Term Capital Gains.
3. For resident individual aged below 60, one could avail 250,000 rupees exemption for Long-Term Capital Gains.
4. For a nonresident individual, irrespective of the age, the exemption limit is 250,000 rupees.

Buying a home

Another important way to levy tax exemptions would be to buy a home or build a home with the acquired capital. It should be done within the fiscal year to avail the tax exemptions in case of buying a home. A period of 3 years is given to build a new home and avail the same tax exemptions.

It should also be noted that the home under construction or the home bought is limited to one home from the capital gains as of 2017 – 2018 and it should not be sold within the following 3 years.

Capital Gains Account Scheme (CGAS)

In case, you are not able to buy the home within the specified span of time, you could deposit the capital gains in a Capital Gains Account Scheme to buy some more time without having to pay the taxes.

To avail any form of exemptions regarding the capital gains, you would have to be a resident Indian.

There are two types of schemes to choose from.

1. Deposit Scheme A
2. Deposit Scheme B

The deposit scheme A behaves like a savings account. The capital gains deposited could be flexibly withdrawn but the interest earned will be equivalent to the bank savings account interest rates.

The deposit scheme B behaves like a term deposit. The Interest earned is much more than the scheme A. But the amount deposited cannot be withdrawn for the specified period of time.

It is worth noting that the interests earned are taxable.

Capital Gains Bond

Exemptions on the long-term capital gains can be availed if you invest the capital gains on the government specified bonds.

The bonds that come under the capital gains are National Highway Authority of India (NHAI) and Rural Electric Corp. (REC). These bonds as of 2017 provide an interest rate of 5.25%. The Capital Gains invested by you will not be taxed if invested in these specified bonds but the gains arising from the interests of these investments are taxable.

A maximum of 5,000,000 rupees can be exempt by investing in these bonds. It is to be noted that this is the aggregated maximum investment allowed in these bonds.

The bonds are issued for a period of 3 years and are non-transferable, non-negotiable and cannot be offered as a security for any loans.

Capital Gains	Rs.5,000,000
Tax @20%	Rs.1,000,000
Interest Rate @5.25% Year 1	Rs.262,500
Interest Rate @5.25% Year 2	Rs.262,500
Interest Rate @5.25% Year 3	Rs.262,500
Total Return on Investment	44.69%
Return on Investment Per Year	14.89%

If you have paid a tax on the capital gains earned, the amount available for investment would be 4,000,000 rupees. Upon investing the taxed capital gains, you would require an annualized return of 14.89% and a total return of 44.69% for 3 years to make up for the losses in taxes and equalize the returns that you would have made by investing in government capital gains bonds.

We have not included educational cess and surcharges on the tax as it depends on the tax slab of every individual. The point to ponder is that taxes are a heavy burden on the investment and you should do everything in your power to avail tax exemptions on the Long Term Capital Gains.

VANGUARD 500 INDEX INVESTOR (VFINX)

The stock prices mentioned above are much accurate for dollar-weighted returns. i.e all the capital is invested in 1988 and then we wait for the investment to reap benefits.

The nominal fund growth of the Vanguard 500 Index Investor (VFINX) is 1352% for 39 years. Your $14.34 would have grown to $208.33. Adjusting for inflation, the real returns of the index fund comes down to 587.64%. Inflation eats away your potential purchase power. The real gain in the purchase value per year is 15% pre-tax and pre-cost deduction.

This is a much realistic return to expect. VFINX has an expense ratio of 0.14% which means that you pay less in fees. You could save about $1913 for every $10,000 invested and end up spending only $329 on fees for a 10 year period.

That's savings in cost of about 678%. In other words, you would pay 678% more in costs alone when you invest with index funds with an industrial average expense ratios.

Assuming a 10 percent return on investment with an expense ratio of 0.14%, you are looking forward to paying 1.4% of the market returns in cost in one year.

COMPARISON OF FUNDS

As the graph below suggests, keeping up with the index is hard. The index is a measure of potential market returns. It is the maximum return anybody can expect to attain by investing in stocks. Index fund tries to attain the market returns and lags by 91%. Even though it lags by that percentage it is 293%

higher than the FFIDX mutual fund's cumulative growth.

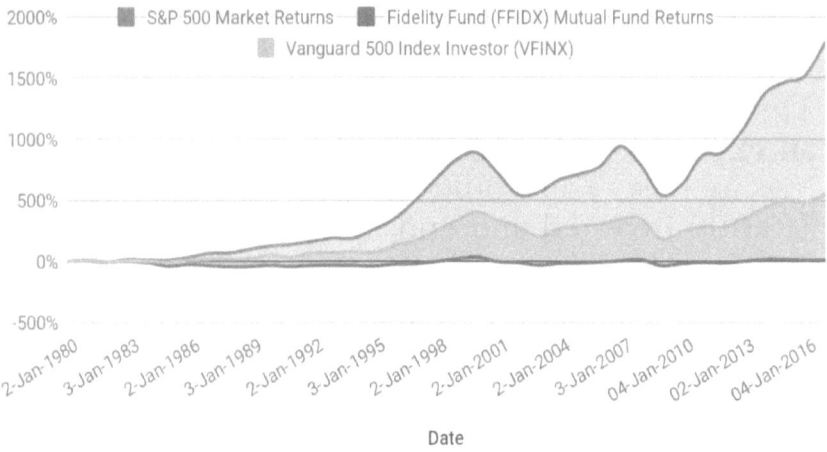

FFIDX lags the potential market returns by a staggering 652%. The mutual fund almost has the same volatility as the market itself. So the best course of action if invested in the mutual fund would be to retrieve the investment during the tech market bubble in the 2000's.

That way, the return on investment would be 200.25% for a 12 year period and the inflation-adjusted returns would yield 111% real return on investment for FFIDX. The market returns for the FFIDX per year would have been 9.25%.

The returns are great for mid-term investment in mutual funds but for the long term, the inflation-adjusted market returns dwindle to a mere 93.383% for a 30 year period from 1988 to 2017. The real returns per year before tax are at an all-time low of 3.11%.

On the other hand, the Vanguard 500 Index Investor (VFINX) fund produces a cumulative growth of 425% for a period of 12 years spanning from 1988 to 2000 which is an inflation-adjusted return of 268%. It would yield a real return of 22.41% per year before tax.

The long-term investment of VFINX is promising as well. The real returns for a period spanning from 1988 – 2017 is 358.12%. The real returns per year would be 11.9% before tax.

PEAK

Though the long-term prospects of Index funds look promising, let's look at the scenarios where the investor buys a stock during the peak and the effect it has on the returns.

Let's say that you have bought the Vanguard 500 Index Investor (VFINX) during the peaks of 2000's and sold it in 2017. The stock price was at $134.03 in 2000 and the stock price was $208.33 in 2017. The nominal return on investment is at a mere 55.4%. The real returns on investment would be 10.4% for a period of 17 years. A real return on investment per year of 0.61% before tax.

Though you haven't lost any money, you haven't earned any money as well. The nominal return of 55.4% was solely earned during the last five years. You would have earned a total real return of $26.39 in total for every share invested in VFINX.

You could have earned 33.52 inflation-adjusted dollars for every share invested in VFINX if you invested in 2015 and sold it in 2017.

These kinds of mistakes can be easily avoided if you follow two simple strategies

1. Buy majority of the shares when there is peak pessimism.
2. Sell majority of the shares when there is peak optimism.

In the end, stock prices are just a reflection of the current mood of the economic future.

> "When the price to earnings ratio of the stock is 7:1, the mood is despair and when the price to earnings ratio of the stock is 21:1, the mood is exuberance" – **John C. Bogle.**

Price to Earnings ratio (P / E) is the price of the stock for every dollar of earning. It can be reliably used to measure the mood of the economy along with what the media and your colleagues have to say about the economic future of the country/stock.

When the majority of the people buy a stock, it's time to sell and when the majority of the people sell their stock, Its time to buy. That's how you get the best deal.

If you do not know anything about the P / E ratio and never intend to learn about it, a simple yet powerful strategy could be used to avoid such mistakes. It's called Dollar Cost Averaging.

It's the act of depositing a set amount of money every month into buying a fund thereby spreading out the potential loss across time. It's the most powerful way to avoid such financial blunders.

HOW COULD THE INDEX FUND BE USED TO AID IN THE ATTAINMENT OF FINANCIAL FREEDOM?

Index funds can be used for several scenarios.

1. It could be used to invest for buying a home in the long run.
2. It must be used for funding your retirement through ROTH IRA or IRA if you are in the US.
3. It could be used to attain your Long Term Dream / Midterm Dream including the ability to fund your children's college education.

While investing in index funds, always look for ways to reduce your tax burden.

29

Investing in Fixed Deposits

Fixed Deposits are one of the most common forms of investment in the developing nations, although not common among developed nations. These play an important role when it comes to managing emergency funds.

They are also the least sort after forms of investments but are a good fit for emergency funds.

EMERGENCY FUND!

Let's get real. We may not need the 12 months worth of income to be available at our disposal all the time.

It should be available in our bank when it is necessary and the invested money should be flexible enough to withdraw /redeposit or avail overdraft when ever demanded.

Fixed deposits make all these possible. They are flexible enough to let you avail overdraft on the fixed deposit without any overdraft charges for 3 months or more.

In most cases, the fixed deposits can be withdrawn immediately with about 1% penalty on the interest rate.

Investing $100,000 for one year with an interest rate of 7%, you will be charged 1% of the interest rate on premature withdrawal.

$100,000 at the rate of 6% interest rate on premature withdrawal by 6 months will yield $3000 on half yearly compounded interest.

Emergency funds need not necessarily yield nil return. Any investment with 100% security and 0% risk with the possibility of withdrawing the money anytime will be a perfect fit.

CATCH UP WITH INFLATION

Growth is necessary for the emergency funds as it has to keep up with the inflation of the economy. We do not want the emergency fund to buy us a little less of something as every year goes by.

The following table assumes an emergency fund of $100,000 under the Fixed Deposit for which the interest rates are compounded half yearly.

Year	1% Interest rate	3% Interest rate	5% Interest rate	7% Interest rate	9% Interest rate
1	$101,002.50	$103,022.50	$105,062.50	$107,122.50	$109,202
2	$102,015.05	$106,136.36	$110,381.29	$114,752.30	$119,251
3	$103,037.75	$109,344.3	$115,969.34	$122,925.53	$130,226
4	$104,070.70	$112,649.26	$121,840.29	$131,680.90	$142,210
5	$105,114.01	$116,054.08	$128,008.45	$141,059.87	$155,296
6	$106,167.78	$119,561.81	$134,488.88	$151,106.8	$169,588
7	$107,232.11	$123,175.57	$141,297.38	$161,869.45	$185,194
8	$108,307.11	$126,898.55	$148,450.56	$173,398.60	$202,237
9	$109,392.89	$130,734.06	$155,965.87	$185,748.92	$220,847
10	$110,489.55	$134,685.50	$163,861.64	$198,978.89	$241,171

As time goes by we can double the initial deposit of emergency fund if the interests are reinvested. As discussed in the previous chapters, you can also use the Albert Einstein's rule of 72 to find out exactly how long it takes for the money to double itself.

While shopping around for higher interest rates in your country, it is also mandatory to check the stability of the banks you are depositing them under.

Fixed Deposit Interest Growth

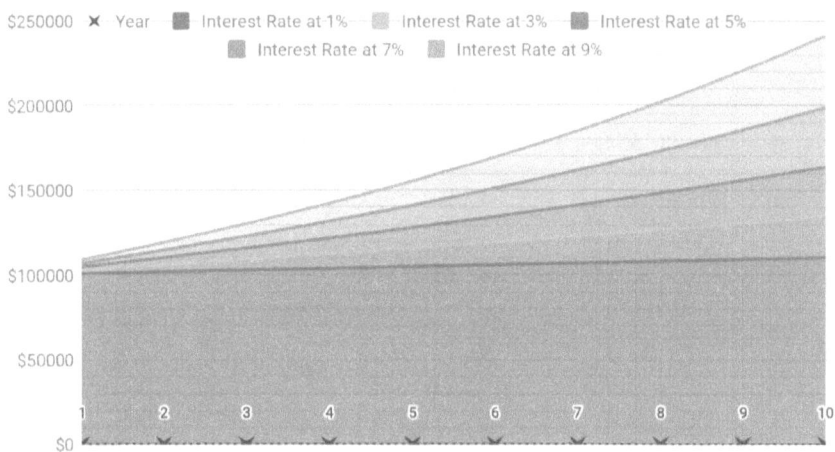

The graphical representation of the growth of emergency funds in fixed deposits for its respective interest rates is shown in the above-mentioned chart.

Lehman Brothers, a bank with a 100-year-old history became bankrupt during the housing market crisis bringing the whole economic system to a standstill. One of the primary factors influencing the stability of a bank is the number of years since inception and how big the bank actually is. But these cannot be reliable measures in recent years as the 2008 housing market crash reminded us.

So it is often better to divide your fixed deposits to a minimum of 2 banks. if possible let one of them be a government-run bank as it gives you an added security.

DO YOU KNOW IF YOU COULD GET YOUR MONEY BACK IF BANKS BECOME BANKRUPT?

In such cases, the US has Federal Deposit Insurance Corporation to take care of the bankruptcy of the bank smoothly. But what about India?

India has Deposit Insurance and Credit Guarantee Corporation (DICGC) which guarantees a maximum of one lakh rupees saved for both principal and interest amount in a bank for each depositor.

Fixed deposit

Fixed deposit interest rates fluctuate. It also depends on every nation and how important the bank plays a role in facilitating the functioning of the economy as a whole.

Developed nations generally provide the least interest rates. It may fluctuate between 1% to as high as 5.5% in Europe, USA, and the UK.

While developing nations interest rate may vary from 6% to as high as 14%.

The general direction the interest rate of the fixed deposit takes when the country transforms from underdeveloped to developing to developed nations is generally downwards.

Historically interest rates were a big attraction to open a bank account. Bank accounts were not mandatory and did not play an important role in the economy as it does today. Hence the primary motivation for any person to open a bank account would be the interest the money earns.

As banks begin playing a majority role in the creation of money, it pays for the government to make the bank account mandatory for every transaction.

As this happens, the banks lose the necessity to provide higher interest rates to attract new bank accounts.

In order to control the flow and the general direction of the economy, interest rates are decided by centralized banks. The central banks play a role in motivating people to either take a loan or to start saving by varying the interest rates.

In 2008, interest rates in majority of the developed nations fell to a rock bottom. As people lose the motivation to take a loan, the money in the economic system starts to dwindle. People stop paying loans and as a result, money disappears from the system.

To prevent this from happening the central bank varies the interest rate to stimulate the economy and provide price stability but during the economic crisis under extreme conditions, the central banks run out of ways to stimulate the economy and the government steps in.

The governments can pump money into the system by providing it to banks/businesses. That way the money seeps into the economy and keeps the money flowing.

When all of the tricks fail, its usual that the growth in the economic system stops, deflation starts to kick in and job cuts become a common phenomenon.

Varying interest rates is not the only way to stimulate the economy. The central banks can also buy back the treasury notes to pump money into the system.

If the inflation stops due to the economic crisis, it is usual that the central banks would have already lowered the interest rates on the bank deposit. So it does not matter what the interest rates for fixed deposits are as it is always in close proximity to the inflation.

What makes more sense is the relation between the fixed deposit interest rates and the inflation of the currency.

This relationship is sure to stay within acceptable limits at least in the developed nations.

So, it doesn't matter if you are in a developed nation or developing nation and if there is an economic crisis in your country or not. Fixed deposits are the best way to ensure your emergency fund stays safe and earns interest at the same time while not destroying the whole purpose of having an emergency fund.

Bibliography

Bach, D. (2016). *Automatic Millionaire*. The Crown Publishing Group.

Bogle, J. (2009). *Enough: True Measures of Money, Business and Life*. John Wiley & Sons.

Branson, R. (2015). *The Virgin Way*. Virgin Publishing.
Carnegie, D. (1981). *How to win friends and influence people*. London: Vermilion.

Clason, G. S. (2017). *The richest man in Babylon*. Place of publication not identified: Dauphin Publications.

COVEY, R. (2013). *7 HABITS OF HIGHLY EFFECTIVE PEOPLE*. Place of publication not identified: SIMON & SCHUSTER LTD.

Eker, T. (2005). *Secrets of the millionaire mind*. New York (210 min.): Harper Audio.

Gladwell, M. (. (2015). *The tipping point: how little things can make a big difference*. London: Abacus.

Gladwell, M. (2013). *Outliers: the story of success*. New York: Back Bay Books.

Goleman, D. (1996). *Emotional intelligence*. London: Bloomsbury.

Goleman, D. (2006). *Social intelligence*. London: Bloomsbury.

Graham, B. (1998). *Security analysis*. New York: McGraw-Hill.

Griffin, G. (2010). *The creature from Jekyll Island*. Westlake Village, CA.: American Media.

Guillebeau, C. (2015). *The $100 startup: fire your boss, do what you love and work better to live more*. London: Pan Books.

Guystuffcounseling.com. (2018). *Facing a Midlife Crisis Divorce*. [online] Available at: https://www.guystuffcounseling.com/counseling-men-blog/facing-a-midlife-crisis-divorce [Accessed 3 Aug. 2018].

HARARI, Y. (2018). *HOMO DEUS*. [S.l.]: MCCLELLAND & STEWART.

Hicks, E., & Hicks, J. (2009). *Law of Attraction – 2010*. Burgrain: KOHA-Verl.

Hill, N. (2017). *The law of success*. NY, NY: TarcherPerigee, an imprint of Penguin Random House LLC.

Hill, N., & Sartwell, M. (2007). *Napoleon Hills keys to success: the 17 principles of personal achievement*. New York: Plume.

Lipton, B. H., & Bhaerman, S. (2012). *Spontaneous evolution: our positive future (and a way to get there from here)*. Carlsbad, CA: Hay House.

Man spends $40,000 buying out IMAX theaters to prove ex-girlfriend wrong. (2018, May 5). Retrieved August 2, 2018, from https://shanghaiist.com/2014/06/26/man-spends-400k-buying-out-imax-theaters/

Money Goals to Reach By Age 35!! (2017, June 7). Retrieved August 2, 2018, from http://www.rashminds.com/2017/06/07/money-goals-to-reach-by-age-35/

Peck, M. S. (1984). People of the lie: the hope for healing human evil. Washington, D.C.: NLS.

Peck, M. S. (2008). The road less traveled: a new psychology of love, traditional values and spiritual growth. London: Rider.

Perdue, C. L. (1987). Outwitting the Devil: Jack tales from Wise County, Virginia. Santa Fe, NM: Ancient City Press.

Ramsey, D. (2009). The total money makeover: a proven plan for financial fitness. Nashville, TN: Thomas Nelson Pub.

Robbins, A. (2013). Awaken the giant within: how to take immediate control of your mental, emotional, physical & financial destiny! New York: Simon & Schuster Paperbacks.

Robbins, T. (2007). Time Of Your Life. Robbins Research International Inc.

Robbins, T. (2014). Money Master the Game. Simon & Schuster.

Schwartz, D. J. (2016). *The magic of thinking big*. London: Vermilion.

Sharma, R. (2017). *The rise and fall of nations: ten rules of change in the post-crisis world*. London: Penguin Books.

Sharma, R. S. (2015). *The monk who sold his Ferrari: a spiritual fable about fulfilling your dreams and reaching your destiny*. London: Thorsons.

'She had millions and she had never mentioned a word'. (2018, May 10). Retrieved August 2, 2018, from https://www.news.com.au/finance/money/wealth/former-secretary-amassed-hidden-12-million-wealth-over-seven-decades/news-story/4c44e26b9a968aff70d91d7fc425a9a9

Soros, G. (2003). *The alchemy of finance*. Hoboken, N.J.: J. Wiley.

Swensen, D. and Bogle, J. (2013). *Common sense on mutual funds*. Hoboken, N.J.: Wiley.

Trading for a living psychology, trading tactics, money management. (2000). Carlsbad, CA: Penton Overseas.

Trump, D. (2007). *Think big and kick ass*. [Place of publication not identified]: Harpercollins.

Wattles, W. (2017). *The Science of Getting Rich*. Lanham: Dancing Unicorn Books.

Investment Advice Disclaimer

In launching this book, I've tried to be as transparent as possible while assuming that you are a reasonable person. To this end, I've been providing my suggestions on personal financial success. They include lifestyle changes, strategy, and point of view changes for the long term before starting your investment journey. They take years to perfect, You will not happily retire in six months to one year after implementing the strategies mentioned throughout the book. I do not promote the get rich quick schemes. Building your personal finance takes time and a lot of effort.

Any advice mentioned in this book has been tried and tested by myself. However, this does NOT GUARANTEE that employing the same techniques, ideas, strategies, products or services I discuss will yield the same result for you. The examples and strategies mentioned in the book are through my personal experience except where mentioned and they have been very effective in upgrading my financial situation. This may or may not work for your specific ideas, implementation, and goals and are not interpreted to be a guarantee of earnings and success.

The materials provided by readorb.com cannot be in any way interpreted as a "Get Rich Quick" schemes. Succeeding in personal finance takes a lot of effort from you and your family. A lot! Your success potential is entirely dependent upon you and the current market situation.

1. Past performance of any funds mentioned in the website does not guarantee future performance.
2. The science of succeeding in personal finance also depends on your current market situation and will not yield the same results for any two individuals.

WHETHER YOU ARE SUCCESSFUL EMPLOYING THESE STRATEGIES AND TECHNIQUES IS DEPENDENT ON FACTORS INCLUDING BUT NOT LIMITED TO YOUR DEDICATION, YOUR PURPOSE OF SAVING, YOU FAMILY SUPPORT IN THE ENDEAVOR, MARKET KNOWLEDGE, AND THE TIME YOU DEVOTE TOWARDS BUILDING YOUR PERSONAL FINANCES. BECAUSE OF THIS, I CANNOT GUARANTEE YOUR FINANCIAL SUCCESS LEVEL.

I can guarantee this much. The resources will be useful to anyone reading this regardless of who they are or where they are from. And that once implemented into their lives will bring about a positive change which you were looking for.

Always remember

> "The right things done at the wrong time is a wrong thing" – **Joshua Harris**

With due apologies for the legal double Dutch, "There are always some people with unrealistic expectations."

Nagarjun Nagesh
nagarjun@readorb.com

www.ingramcontent.com/pod-product-compliance
Lightning Source LLC
Chambersburg PA
CBHW031614210526
45464CB00004B/1576